T0129580

The Sheep GATE

BRIAN HORST

WESTBOW
PRESS®
A DIVISION OF THOMAS NELSON
& ZONDERVAN

Scripture quotations are from The Holy Bible, English Standard Version® (ESV®), copyright © 2001 by Crossway, a publishing ministry of Good News Publishers. Used by permission. All rights reserved.

WestBow Press books may be ordered through booksellers or by contacting:

WestBow Press
A Division of Thomas Nelson & Zondervan
1663 Liberty Drive
Bloomington, IN 47403
www.westbowpress.com
1 (866) 928-1240

ISBN: 978-1-5127-1979-6 (sc)
ISBN: 978-1-5127-1980-2 (hc)
ISBN: 978-1-5127-1978-9 (e)

Library of Congress Control Number: 2015919086

Print information available on the last page.

WestBow Press rev. date: 11/23/2015

Contents

The Questions

The wise man seeks wisdom; knowledge is mocked by the fool
Strength is given to the meek, hardships come to the cruel

We all have questions about this life. We wonder why certain things happen and other things don't. We wonder why this person has such a great life and we don't. We wonder what the after life is all about. We wonder how to get through this life. We wonder why things are so difficult. I can't answer all these questions. But I can, hopefully, help you get to a point in life where these questions won't affect you anymore. I hope to help you find peace with this life, with the people around you and, especially, with yourself. I hope to help you be content with this life and feel the love God has for you.

First I have to ask you this question. Have you ever felt like you aren't good enough? Have you ever felt like you are useless, worthless, and shameful or just feel bad about yourself? Guess what you aren't good enough and, sorry to tell you, you never will be, not on your own but don't worry God loves you. God loves you exactly the way you are. He isn't even asking you to change. He loves you and everyone else with all his love. In other words nothing you do will make him love you more or less. He wants to help you. All that he is asking you to do is turn to him, ask for help and let him do the rest. Put your life in his hands so he can give you the life he has waiting just for you. Then he can make you the person he created you to be. Then all those lies of self doubt will disappear and you will find peace. Will life always be easy? No. Will things always go the way you think they should? Of course not but God will help you through it all and show you how to deal with life and all the things that come with it. All that he asks of you is to put your faith in Jesus Christ, love him, and no matter what happens in life, always try.

Why is it we feel this way about ourselves at different times in our life? Why is it we do things we truly feel like we shouldn't? Why is it these horrible things happen in life? What is it we can do to get on, what people call,

"The right track"? These are some more questions I hope to answer. But before I go any further please understand that no one is actually useless or worthless or any of these types of things. These are all lies Satan feeds to us. The more you doubt yourself the easier it is for him to tempt you. He wants to be your master, he wants control.

Imagine holding a piece of rotting fruit in your hand. We'll use a peach for this example. Really imagine this, hold your hand out and a look at the fruit. Now tell that fruit to look nicer, smell better, to do its one job and be edible, and to get rid of those brown and white spots, stop being gross and start being perfect. What is the only thing that is going to happen as you speak to this piece of fruit? It's only going to rot a little more, that's all it will do. What happens when we do this to ourselves? When we tell ourselves to look better, be nicer, stop swearing, stop being gross, do a better job, be as good a person as that person is etc. The only thing that happens is we rot a little more. The more we try to change ourselves on our own the worse we become. The more we focus on the things we need to change the less we focus on God. This is exactly what Satan wants. He wants us turned away from God so he can rule over us. Remember there are only two ways to live. Either you are following Satan or you have faith in Christ. That's it, one or the other. We are always serving a master. Either one who loves us and wants to help us or one who just wants to control us.

The first big question is "What is sin?" The word sin actually comes from an old archery term. When archers would practice shooting at targets they would set the target so far away that they couldn't see where the arrow hit. So they would have their helper stand by the target. If the arrow missed the bulls-eye the helper would yell back to the archer "Sin". Sin is being just off the mark. Sin puts us just off the mark of God's perfection. If we could always put God first in our lives, always follow his commandments and always listen to his guidance, do God's will, we would be perfect, but as Paul says in Romans 3:11-12 "No one is righteous, no not one." In other words, no one can do these things. Each and every one of us is just off of God's mark. This makes each one of us equal, none better or worse than the other. From Adolf Hitler to Martin Luther King Jr; from Charles Manson to Charlie Chaplin; we are all equal. We are all sinners.

What is a sinner? A sinner, of course, is someone who sins. We don't sin all the time. I'm only known as a driver when I'm in my car and it's moving, not when I'm riding a bike or taking a walk. Think of someone like Michal Jordan or Mike Tyson, anyone famous, when you hear the name Michal Jordan or even see him on a Hanes commercial you think of him as a basketball player. The same with Tyson or Ali, you always think of them as a boxer regardless of what they're doing at the time. Any well known professional is thought of as their profession. We are "professional" sinners. We will never stop sinning. Whether we move, get a new job, get married, hit the lottery, go to the moon or whatever, we will be sinners. We are born sinners and only through God's grace and our faith can we be forgiven for that. When we are forgiven and we are saved we become "retired" sinners. We still sin but we try not to do it as much as we used to. Just like anyone who had a long career. Chances are when they do retire from their career they are still going to do whatever it was they had been doing but just not as much. Take a chef for example. I'm sure a chef would still cook for friends and family but not for the public. So he still cooks just not as much as he had before retirement. As I said we will always be sinners but after we are saved we truly don't want to sin. In the book of John and in chapter 8 Jesus is brought to him a woman who had been caught in the act of adultery. The men who brought the woman to Jesus wanted to stone her. Jesus explained to them why they shouldn't stone her. After Jesus convinces the men not to stone her he tells the woman to go and sin no more. To read the full story go to John 8:3-11. This is what Jesus is saying to all of us "Go and sin no more." After we are saved we are no longer slaves to sin, we no longer automatically sin. We are set free from it and now we have a choice to sin or not to sin. And all of our sins are forgiven through Jesus shedding his blood for us and our faith in him.

Where did sin come from? If God is perfect how did things become this way? God created a perfect world where all things lived together and worked together in harmony. God made man to basically be the caretakers of that creation. He wanted to give us everything we would need to accomplish that and to live in harmony. But he also gave us free will. Free will is the ability to make choices for ourselves. He wanted and wants us to choose to love him, not be forced to. Think about when you're starting something new maybe you start playing a new sport or instrument or start a new job or whatever, you want someone to tell you how you are doing. You want someone to tell you that you are doing good but you don't want to ask them because then they will probably tell you that you're doing good, not because that's what they think but because you ask. When you ask someone they are more or less forced to tell you your doing good, they didn't choose to tell you that. When they just come up to you and say "Hey nice job," you know they're being honest. God wants us to choose to tell him we love him, not be forced to.

I'll go into more details about the fall of man later but these are the basics. In the Garden of Eden God told Adam and Eve they may eat of any tree they wanted except one. Then Satan came along and said "Really, I don't think he would mind if you ate of that tree. Did he really say you couldn't, maybe you misunderstood what he meant." Not in those exact words but something along those lines. So they ate of that tree. That's when they learned the knowledge of good and evil and realized they didn't have to follow God's will.

Sin is going against God's will for us. Sin separates us from God. Now we know both good and evil. First Adam and Eves natural instinct was to do God's will but when they learned they had a choice they turned away from God and only focused on themselves. Death is what is earned because of sin. Death is eternal separation from God but God doesn't want us to be separated from him, he loves us. Remember he gave Adam and Eve paradise to live in and they choose to lose that. God is perfection and can not have evil in his presence. Like when your child, if you have kids, goes against something you tell them to do. You might be very upset for a while but you will always love them. God has unconditional love for us. No matter what we do he will always love us and God already knows every choice we are going to make. He has already seen it all. We still have to make the choices; he just knows what's going to happen. God could have simply destroyed us but he loves us and wants us with him. When Adam and Eve were removed from the Garden of Eden they were cursed by the evil they learned. Sin is that curse. We all still live with that curse. Sin simply is being just off of God's mark of perfection which causes us to be separated from him which causes death. Our choice, simply, is to either put our faith in Christ and be reconnected with God and then have eternal bliss or face eternal separation from God in hell.

When we put our faith in Christ we see how life changes, we experience God's plan and the only thing we need to do is give ourselves to God. We just need to love him and listen to what he is telling us to do. We've all, at different times, lived our life our way. But what does that get us?

We feel unhappy and it feels like something is missing in are lives. Some of us get to the point of giving up on life. I personally got very close to that myself. You feel incomplete. You feel like you can't accomplish anything in this life. You get to a point where you feel like life has no purpose. You've tried and tried and all you do is fail. Guess what when you try things without God you probably will fail. I don't mean all the time but things are so much harder without God's guiding hand there to help show you the way. We all need God. He will get your thoughts straight, make you feel whole and fill you up completely. He will give you the things you need to get through this life. The best way to put it is with God all things are possible. Look at Mat. 19:26 and you will see that is what Jesus says.

The biggest question is why do you have a life? What is the purpose of life? Why are we born if we are just going to die anyway? Think about this, God made each and every single one of us. None of us were born by accident. So the true question is why did God put us here, why did God put YOU here? Though we are all sinners, though we all make stupid mistakes and though we all have major faults God loves us, all of us. God wants YOU here on this earth and he has a purpose, a reason, for you to be here. Whenever you feel completely alone remember God is with you always. Not sometimes or here and there but ALWAYS. That is what Jesus says in Mat. 28:20. God wants to help you just turn to him and ask. Or in other words put your faith in him and pray. Now God can show you a new way to live. Through the grace that Jesus has brought us we are set free and now live under God's promises. He promises us that through faith in Jesus we will live in eternal bliss with him and have everything we ask for that is true to God's plans, not your own plans, in this life.

Ask yourself if life would be better or worse with Jesus in it? What would truly change in your life? What's the worst thing that could happen if you put your faith in Jesus? Truly think about these things and remember God loves you just the way you are. You don't have to change anything for him. The only thing God wants from you is what you want from life and that, quite simply, is love.

The true answers to all of our questions are found in the bible. The Holy Bible is God's true word written through the inspiration he gave to different men. The bible is a road map for life. I used to wish someone would give me a book or something like that to show me how to get through this thing we call life. I didn't believe there was such a thing until I started to read God's word. If you want help getting through this life open up a bible and see for yourself what it has to say and how it will truly change your view of things. No one has ever said life is easy and I don't think anyone ever will. But when you open those pages and start a relationship with God life becomes so much more, you feel his Holy Spirit inside you and there are no words to describe how that feels. You lose absolutely nothing by putting your faith in Christ. But if you never turn to him you will never know what this life has to offer. You will never know what it's like to feel peace. You will never know what it's like to love yourself and everyone around you. It's impossible for you to be content with your life without having God be the most important thing in it.

God is the creator of this whole entire universe. He knows all, sees all and can make anything happen. He created all the planets, the stars, the oceans, the mountains, the dry land, every single thing in this universe. And yet the most important thing to him is YOU. He wants you to know him. He knows everything about you and loves you. He knows all the stupid things you've done but still loves you and just wants you to love him back and never give up, always try. Every single day is a new day to start over and try again. Never forget God, the creator of everything we see, wants nothing more than for us to love him. Turn to God ask for help put your trust in him and he will show you how much he loves you.

The Spiral of Fear and Circle of Love

A child can only learn what you teach
Like a thirsty man and the well is just out of reach

The next big question is what is life? My personal answer is life is choices. We have so many choices to make in life and usually we make the wrong ones. Thankfully, God knows all things. He knows the choices we are going to make and he will make it all work out. He can't control our choices but he can help us get through them and make everything work out for our better. We make a mistake and God teaches us a lesson. We don't always see what God is trying to teach us. We usually go through a process. We usually make the same mistake a few times until we learn a lesson or at least realize we need to change what we are doing but just because we realize we're doing something we think is wrong or stupid doesn't mean we'll stop and quite often we can't stop. Thankfully, that's where God steps in. He makes us realize we are doing something that affects our lives in a negative way and he helps us stop doing these things. We are going to take a closer look at sin and why it affects our lives the way it does.

We are now going to talk about the act of sinning. Remember we are born sinners but through our actions we still sin, we still go against God's will for us. He tells us not to eat the apple and we do it anyway. Usually we do whatever it is we are told not to do. I know this very well from my own personal experiences. Keep in mind I never said I was smart but I've learned a lot and continue to learn thanks to God's guiding hand. God knows what things are the best for our lives. We have no idea. We'd like to think and pretend we do but in all honesty we just have wants and desires. When we go against God's will for us we are doing the action of sinning. We are already sinners but now we are involved in doing the deed. As I mentioned before we are professional sinners. We are known as sinners all the time but when we sin we our actually playing the game. Back to my Michael Jordan example; he is known as a basketball player all the time but he is only playing ball during the games. How do we know when we've sinned? We feel guilt and sometimes shame. This is a mental and emotional response. Every action in life has both a mental process and an emotional response. First you think about something and then you choose to act on it. For example if a baseball player is up to bat he is first thinking "Swing," which is the mental process. The emotional response would depend on if he hit the ball and how well he hit it. When looking at a women lustfully the mental process would be thinking of things you want to do with her that are impure. The emotional response would be the feeling you get from having those thoughts. Jesus says in Mat. 5:28 "Anyone who looks at a women with lustful intent has already committed adultery with her is his heart." Satan puts many crazy thoughts and many temptations in our heads but unless we act on those thoughts we haven't sinned. To look at a woman lustfully is to act on your thoughts. You can look at a woman and see that she is attractive or you can look at her and think of all the impure things you'd like to do with her. Sin is an action and by looking at a woman in a lustful way you are acting on your thoughts because you have the choice to turn away or to keep on looking but that is up to you.

With the action of sinning the mental process is guilt. When you sin, when you act out your thought, you first know in your mind what you did was wrong, you "Broke the rules." That doesn't mean you feel bad about it, you know it was wrong and you shouldn't have done that but you don't actually feel bad about it. For example if someone robs a gas station they know that it was wrong, it's something you shouldn't do but that doesn't necessarily mean they feel bad about it. That's just the first response to it. That is the mental process, which is guilt, knowing you did something you shouldn't have done.

The next step is the emotional response to sin which is shame. After you mentally process sin and think about guilt your emotions take over and you feel ashamed of yourself, you feel bad for what you've done. Whether we realize it or not we always feel shame. We don't always allow the feeling of shame to present its self in us. We push it down deep inside but it does always effect us in some way. When you combine the mental process- guilt, with the emotional response- shame, you get that lovely little thing called regret. Guilt + Shame= Regret. You know what you did was wrong and feel bad about it so now you wish you wouldn't have done it. You wish you could take it back but you can't. So, naturally, you start to blame others and you start making excuses for what you've done. Let's go back to the gas station example. After you rob a gas station you might think something like if my wife wouldn't have made me late for work I wouldn't have lost my job and had to rob that store just to pay the rent. It's always if so and so wouldn't have done this then I wouldn't have had to do that. Or if this, this and this wouldn't have happened I wouldn't have had to do this. It's always easier to make excuses than to see we had other options. We always have another choice, always. After you blame others or make excuses usually you will receive some sort of punishment. In some way everything you do has a consequence. You could have legal punishment, such as a prison sentence, or maybe some other person is punishing you, telling you everything is your fault and how bad of a person you are. Or the most common punishment is self punishment, you beat yourself up for the things you've done. You tell yourself how horrible you are and how this isn't normal, most people wouldn't do this, and maybe you feel worthless. Every wrong deed has its result. Usually once you are punished, in whatever form, you feel upset, empty and there's a void you need to fill. So to comfort yourself, to fill that empty feeling, you might get drunk, do drugs, over eat, stay busy in the garden, watch TV or whatever it is that makes you happy for a moment or takes your mind off things. We do these things instead of turning to God and asking him for help. We are putting these things before God in our lives. God should be first in our lives. Turn to him and he will help but what we usually do at this point is just sin again. This starts a spiral in our lives. This is what I call "The Spiral of Fear." We sin and mentally know that what we did was wrong which causes guilt; we feel bad about what we did which is shame; and then we regret doing it and blame others or make excuses for why it happened. That leads to some kind of punishment which makes us feel empty; we need to fill that void, so we usually sin again.

Spiral of Fear- Sin-Guilt-Shame-Regret-Excuses/Blame-Punishment-Emptiness-Sin.

We all get caught in that spiral at some point in our lives. This is exactly what Adam went through in the Garden of Eden. First he sinned by going against what God told him to do. Then he had guilt so he hid himself from God. Have you ever hid yourself from God? Will you want to hide when Christ returns? Christ is the Lamb of God. He is the door we walk through to be saved. Take that first step and walk through the sheep gate, put your faith in Christ, and see how much life will change. It truly is amazing.

While Adam was hiding God ask him why he was hiding and he said because he felt shame, I don't think it was just because he was naked, he knew what he did was wrong in God's eyes. Obviously he regretted it once he saw God's anger. Then he tried to blame both Eve and God. Adam says to God "The woman, who you gave to me, gave me the fruit." God then punished both Adam and Eve for their disobedience. They were then disconnected from God and I'm sure they felt quite an empty void inside. Mankind, in general, still feels that void and is searching for anything to fill it. Did Adam and Eve follow God's commands after they were punished? No. So they both sinned again. That is the "Spiral of Fear."

The question now is how do we stop this spiral? We know when we are on a path to destruction. What do we do to stop from spiraling farther down, out of control. I have said to people that I was on the bottom and still I fell. I thought I had hit rock bottom but I managed to continue to spiral and fall even farther. What can we do to stop this?

Realize that the "Spiral of Fear" is Satan's game. Remember Satan wants us to feel regret and shame. It's much easier to tempt us when we feel bad about ourselves. The true question is how do we stop Satan? That has an easy answer, Jesus Christ. We can only stop Satan with the protection of Jesus. The first step we need to take is to ask for help, ask God to help us. He can show us a new path. He can teach us how to love ourselves. We can't truly love God or anyone else until we understand how to truly love ourselves. I say truly love because we can fake it. We all have faked it at one point or another. Whether it was trying to love others or trying to love God, we loved them to benefit ourselves in some way, not to help them but to help ourselves. This is fake love. When you don't love yourself you need someone else to make you happy, make you feel good. Whether or not you make them happy doesn't matter as long as you get what you want. We do this with God too but of course he already knows what's going on, he knows you don't truly love him but we try to make deals with God. If I give all this stuff to these people then God should give me a bunch of stuff in return. If I bless them God should bless me. You aren't truly worried about helping others you are just getting rid of some things you don't need anymore and hoping you'll get some new things in return. To love God is to obey God; to obey God is to love others. Christ says "Love others as you love yourself." You can't love others until you love yourself and if you don't love others you aren't obeying God and if you aren't obeying God you don't love God. Remember love God above all things and he will make it all work out. Also remember loving God isn't about the things you do, you don't earn God's love, he already loves you, just turn to him and ask for help and he will show you the way. We are born into Satan's world and he is the king of this world and we our born under his power. God wants us to ask for help and to turn from Satan and turn to God. That is to repent. We need help to get out of Satan's grip. We can't "Please" God. He already loves us as much as he can. He wants to help us and that's it. The best way for God to help us is through other people. That is one of many reasons God wants us to give to others and to help others. He wants to save us, to be our savior and to set us free from being slaves to Satan and slaves to sin. He wants us to be able to live, just live and look forward to that wonderful Promised Land which is heaven.

God will show you that in every situation in life there is always a choice. We need to take responsibility for our choices. We need to realize what we did was our fault. We made that decision, that choice. That's why it is said that Adam committed the first sin. Eve ate of the fruit first and then gave it to Adam to eat but Adam had a choice. He didn't have to eat of the fruit he choose to. When you are stuck in the "Spiral of Fear" and you get to the point where you want to blame other people for what they have done turn to yourself and look at what you have done. Understand that you made the choice and you are at fault, you ate the fruit, and no one forced you to do it. Many times when we realize we are at fault we start to regret what we've done. In Genesis 6:6 it says "The Lord regretted that he had made man on the earth and it grieved him to his heart." God regretted making man and now was going to have to destroy them. Most people think that regret comes from sin. How can regret come from sin if God himself regrets things? Think about this, regret comes from you making a choice and it not turning out the way you thought it would. Regret comes from problems and troubles. God obviously knew what was going to happen. He regretted that he was going to have to destroy what he loved. He didn't like what he was going to have to do even though he knew he had to do it. He gave us an example of what to do when things happen that make us feel regret. That is to fix it. We all make mistakes its how we deal with those mistakes that makes all the difference. Things are going to happen in life that you don't expect. It might be from some thing you did or it might not be. But either way it's how we react to those moments that will change our life. Once you realize that you are the one who made a mistake you can confess it to God but first you need Christ's help. You need him to help you love you. To have true freedom in Christ is to have the ability to choose to sin or not to. Before you are set free in Christ you are a slave to Satan. When you are a slave, of any kind, you don't have the ability to make choices. With Christ you are completely set free and now you can choose what you want to do. When you love yourself, through the love Christ has shown you, you love others and you can see what you are doing to the people around you.

To get out of the "Spiral of Fear" ask Christ for help, realize it's your own fault from the choices you made and then confess it to God. When you take responsibility for your own decisions you can confess your wrongs, your sins, to God. When you confess your sins to God it opens you up to him as well as him to you. You have a communication line to and from God. Understand that God is already talking to you but you haven't been talking back and that means you can't feel God when he is talking to you. God asks "Where are you?" just like he did in the garden with Adam. Adam hid from God because he was naked and ashamed. Admit to God that you are afraid, naked and ashamed. Confess all things to him. He already knows it all anyway he just wants to hear you say it. He wants you to admit it to yourself. When God calls just say "Here I am." That is what Abraham did when God called to him. Abraham followed God's direction and God blessed him. Abraham did things his own way sometimes and made mistakes. But God made it all work out because Abraham put his faith in God. So just open up to God and let him lead you. When you have confessed to God he will help make it so that your heart is no longer hardened and he can start to teach you things. Now as you pray (which really just means talk) to God he will start to show and teach you many new things. He will show you the things that are destructive in your life. He will make these things stand out in your mind. When you start to really think about these things you are admitting to yourself, confessing to yourself, that these things are a problem and need to change. The first step to quitting is admitting you have a problem.

As God teaches you, you start to learn from him. You gain new wisdom and understanding. From this new knowledge you start to grow. You become closer to the person God created you to be and you begin following the path toward Christ. Remember that path to destruction you were on? Now you are on the road toward Christ. That is the true goal. God wants us to be the person he created us to be which also gets us closer to being like Christ. The goal truly is to be on the road that leads us there because we can never truly be like Christ until he returns. As you grow, you will feel this peace inside. Though life is tough you just know everything will be okay. You can feel this wonderful steadfast love inside you. That is the Spirit of God, the Holy Spirit. The peace you feel helps to build your relationship with God. The more you build your relationship with God, with Christ, the closer you get and the closer you feel to God, and then you start to trust him. When you trust God you want to talk to him even more. Just like any relationship you have. When you trust someone you want to open up to that person so much more. So when you trust God you will confess that much more to him. This is also how you know that your relationship with Christ is getting stronger. The stronger the relationship the more you talk to him and the more you are willing to open up.

This is what I call the "Circle of Love." Confess your sins to God to open your heart to him, he starts to teach you and you start learning which helps you grow, you are then filled with a feeling of peace from the Holy Spirit which gives you a closer relationship with God and you start to trust him, open up to him and confess that much more.

Circle of Love- Confess-Be Taught-Learn-Grow- Feel Peace-Build Relationship-Trust-Confess

This is the "Spiral of Fear" and the "Circle of Love." Now the only question for you is which do you feel would help you make a better and more enjoyable life for yourself? Don't get me wrong life will always be tough but wouldn't it be nice if there was always someone there to help you get through it? God is **always** there for you, **Always**. Simply ask.

Suffering

The man who stole of course is the thief
The man who seeks revenge will be filled with grief

*T*he biggest question for a lot of people is if there is a loving God why is there so much suffering in this world? I'm going to try to answer that question the best I can. I don't have all the answers; none of us knows it all. Only God knows why all things happen. We, of course, question these things but think about this, how many times a day do you question yourself for the choices you have made? Remember God sees the whole picture. He sees from the beginning of time to the end of time. He knows everything that has and will happen. We see through a tiny little pinhole. Are lives are very short and we only experience the things that we go through. We can't see life through anyone else's eyes. God see's it all, has seen it all and knows what is still to come, yet we still question his decisions. Do we know what is the right or the best thing for us or anyone else? It's kind of like watching a football game on TV and telling the coach and the referees all the things they're doing wrong. We only see what's on the screen they see the whole picture.

Sometimes God is just trying to get our attention, he starts by tapping us on the shoulder. Maybe a friend or family member will say something like "What you are doing you should stop or change." They will say something along those lines. He might put something on our hearts that makes us want to change but we just can't. If that doesn't get your attention then God has to do something more dramatic and he has to slap you across the face to wake you up. He might do something that you feel hurt by and makes you question everything but now you need to turn to him. That is all he wanted from the beginning, he just wants us to turn to him. I personally had to go to jail for a little while. I thought it was the worst thing that could ever happen but it made me reevaluate my life. It gave me a chance to start over and this time I did it with God instead of doing it on my own, my own way. No matter what happens or comes your way God will always be there to help you get through it. Just have faith in him and trust him. Always ask him for help. Don't expect things to be easy. If our lives were simple and easy we wouldn't have a need for God. Life itself is a struggle, but God knows everything we go through, and he is there to show us the way. Think about either watching your own kids learning how to ride a bike or when you learned how to ride a bike. You can't learn without falling a few times. None of us wants to see our kids get hurt but it's the only way to learn. When your child gets hurt you are the one who is there to heal their wounds, to kiss their boo-boo. God doesn't enjoy watching us go through painful events but he is our father and he knows it's the only way we will learn and he is there to heal our wounds, whether they are physical, mental or emotional, he will kiss it and make it all better. Plus Satan is the ruler of this world and he tries very hard to get us to turn to him and turn away from God.

We all need to try to be prepared for things. We need to try to get ready for what ever our next step is going to be. Look in the book of Joshua in chapter 2. Joshua sends spies into Jericho. Why did Joshua send these spies into Jericho? He was preparing to move everyone into the land God had given to them. Sending spies was the best way to be prepared for what lied ahead. Just like Joshua did we all need to be prepared. Every step in life involves some type of preparation. If we want a new job we have to prepare ourselves for it. At least that's the best way to make it happen. The big question is how often are we prepared? Very honestly we are rarely prepared. Say you lose your job out of the blue one day for whatever reason.

What would you do? I'm guessing you would probably be very concerned and you might break down completely. After that, or even during it, I suggest that you talk to God. Pray to him and ask him for help. There might be a beautiful rainbow with a pot of gold and the perfect job waiting at the end but I kind of doubt it. But God will prepare you from that point, just ask. We can not prepare for anything without God doing it for us. He will put us through situations in this life that help prepare us for other major events that are going to happen. God will prepare us.

Along with being prepared for things we most also have patience. Not many of us have patience. I know I don't but God is teaching me, through his confusing ways, how to be more patient. One example of patience is in Joshua chapter 6 through chapter 7. Joshua and the nation of Israel are given Jericho. God instructs them not to plunder anything. God doesn't what them to take a thing from Jericho. In 6:19 it says "All the silver and gold and every vessel of iron shall go into the treasury of heaven." They are to give it all to God. God tells them to burn everything and slaughter all the people and animals. They shouldn't keep anything for themselves. But a man named Achan decided to take a few things. He took some gold and some silver that were about a years worth of wages. The Lord was very upset about this. When the people found out what Achan had done he was stoned to death. After that happened Joshua and the Israelites were given the city of Ai. This time the Lord told them to plunder. He told them to take whatever you want to. Have patience. Listen to God and follow him. You never know what he has waiting just for you. The point here is basically if you have patience you won't be stoned to death. Honestly if you learn through the Holy Spirit and through God's word how to have patience many good things will come to you and life will be much better.

Let's take a look at Jude 10, which says "These people blaspheme all that they do not understand, and they are destroyed by all that they, like wild animals, understand instinctively." Jude is speaking of false teachers. False teachers are anyone who goes against what God's true word says, whether they interpret something wrong and teach others or they simply don't believe God's words and teach against him. This is basically anyone who doesn't understand true biblical doctrine. Honestly we are all false teachers until we give our lives to God. We, as humans, are wild animals without the guidance of the Lord. We need to be trained. We need to be taught how to be lovable so we can obtain God's full love and blessings. So in return we can fully love him. God loves us and is teaching us how to be lovable. The Lord is our shepherd otherwise we are just wild animals living by our own "wild" instincts. When God teaches us we learn how to live by our tamed "trained" instincts. But our natural instinct is to do what we desire not what God's will is for us. As Paul says in Romans 7:24

"What a wretched man I am" and from 7:21 - 23 Paul says he wants to do what is right but sin is always close. In Romans 7:15 he says "I do not understand my own actions. For I do not do what I want, but I do the very thing I hate." As humans we are only flesh and we serve the law of sin. When we put our faith in Jesus Christ and are saved we become covered with the Holy Spirit and the Holy Spirit lives in us. Now we are set free from the law of sin and have the ability to choose to sin or not to sin. No longer are we slaves to Satan, slaves to sin, but we are free in Christ, free from sin. There are no words in this world that sound better than those.

Understand that originally in the Garden of Eden Adams natural instinct was to do God's will. He didn't have to think about it or question anything. This was the only way he knew how to live, it was his natural instinct. But when Satan tempted him and he ate of the apple the Lord had said not to eat of, he learned good and evil. You can't have good without evil and you can't have evil without good. Adam learned both good and evil. Originally all he and Eve knew was God's will. So good and evil are sort of the same thing. Good and evil are over on the left side while God's will is on the right side. Adam and Eve learned how to go against God's will. They learned they could choose whether to listen to God or not to.

Jesus, who is called the "New Adam," was in perfect tune with God's true will. Just as Adam had disconnected man from God through sin, Jesus reconnected man to God by paying the debt of every sin every human being has or will ever commit. Jesus, who never sinned, became sin to save us all. Sin itself is a curse and Jesus became that curse to save us. Jesus was in perfect communication with God. Take a look at Luke 4:3. After Jesus had fasted for 40 days Satan tempted him to turn a rock into bread, which it probably would have been good for Jesus to eat something at that point but that was not God's will for him. God doesn't want any of us to listen to Satan. God always has a better plan for us. We just have to choose to listen to him. Jesus answered Satan by quoting Deuteronomy 8:3 "Man shall not live on bread alone." Jesus gives us a great example here. Whenever Satan is trying to temp you to do things you own way, on your own, quote scripture because Satan is powerless against it. Do you want to live life your own way, alone? So which do we choose good and evil or God's true will?

No longer do we just instinctively do God's will. We have to ask for it and choose it. What is God's will? What is it that we would do differently and how different would the world be if we would do God's will? Does God just want us to listen to everything he tells us because he wants to be in control and have power? No. Is God just trying to show us that we are wrong? No. That's why he gave us free will. He wants us to have the ability to make our own choices. He wants us to choose him. Though God knows the outcome of all of our decisions, we still make the choices. God is teaching us through experience to turn to him so that we are easier to love and in return will have a more stable life. When I say easier to love I don't mean he will love us more. I mean he can give us the things we need if we learn how to receive them. C.S. Lewis talks about this in his book "The Problem of Pain." I'm not quoting him but using his idea. If you have ever had any type of pet you know what it is like to train them. Some are easy, some are very difficult. Every pet has to be trained differently. You have to train your pet where to get food and water, where to go to the bathroom, what yard to stay in, what toys to chew on and not eat, to stay off the couch and the bed, not to bite and many other little things. Ask yourself this question, do you really love your pet more as they learn or are they just easier to love? When you first get a pet usually you love them right away and as they learn the things you teach them they become much easier to love. You don't love them more but now they are part of the family and they know what you expect of them. This is what God is doing for us. When we put our faith in Christ we receive the Holy Spirit. The Holy Spirit teaches us how to live. It teaches us how to love ourselves so that in return we can love others. Remember Jesus says "Love your neighbor as you love yourself." So it is impossible to love others if you are ashamed of yourself. Forgive yourself then you can begin to forgive others. Also realize we do have a conscience, we know right and wrong, but we also don't forget our wrong. Forgive yourself for the things you have done but don't forget what you've done. Life is about learning through experience. If you take a test in school and forget everything the teacher taught you you're probably going to fail. If you remember the things you've done and how they affected you, you won't want to go back to your old life, your "Egypt." You are set free from your old life just as the Israelites were set free from Egypt. In Exodus God sets the Israelites free from Egypt and they praise him for that. But when they are brought out of Egypt they start doubting God. They tell him how much easier it was in Egypt, in their old life. Do you want to continue moving forward in your new life with God or go back to your old life and be a slave to Satan? The walk with God can be very challenging, but it is also very exciting and God will never leave you. He will always teach you new thing so that you can continue to grow and learn how to love.

The world would be a completely different place if everyone wanted to help each other and everyone knew how to receive help. When I say help each other I don't mean just give whatever another person asks for but teach each other how to live. Learn from one another. Do you give a man food for a day or teach him how to grow a garden? That is the basic idea. If we give everything people ask for they don't learn responsibility or they just keep asking and wonder why you can't keep giving.

So what is God's true will for man? To obey him, which really means to love him. What do we need to do to love God? Share him with anyone we can. There is a feeling of peace that comes inside of you when the Holy Spirit comes to you. That is all I want for everyone. I want everyone to know that some how things will be okay. That is the feeling you get when you learn to love God. You know he will provide. That, in a nutshell, is faith. Just knowing God is always there and helping you. Though we will always question his ways, some how it does always work out for our better.

Let me give you an example of what it means to love God. Imagine as a parent that your child stopped paying attention to their favorite T.V. show, band, sport, car, doll, etc. Their life. Then, out of the blue, started telling you how much they love you and how wonderful you are as a parent. How would it make you feel if they told you that you are truly the best parent ever and they love you with all their heart and they have written poems and songs for you and it all truly comes from the heart? Plus they are helping their sibling with their homework and helping to clean the house. If your child helped you do your work and told you how much they loved you and how awesome of a parent you are, sincerely, would it bother you if they messed up sometimes? It might, and all that you would want to do is show them and help them do it right the next time. God loves us 100x this example. He wants us to love him and do his work while he teaches us how to live. Doing his work is helping others. Helping others with their needs and showing them God. Loving him is giving up our self will to him. It's not changing or trying to be good. It's just being us and focusing on Christ and those around us. Christ isn't worried about us messing up. If he were I don't think he would have gone through all that crucifixion trouble.

In general there are 2 main things that cause suffering. The first is our own self doubt. We feel like we aren't good enough, like we are worthless and we can't forgive ourselves for the things we've done in this life. When we beat our self up it causes a lot of inner turmoil and a lot of pain which brings on many crazy thoughts. I can say these things because I've been there and it's horrible and I thank God that I'm on the other side of that now.

The second main reason for suffering is us wanting something someone else has or somebody wanting something we have. These things are called envy or jealousy. This is how every war gets started, why most murders happen, why things get stolen and where most hate comes from. Think about it, would we hate anyone if they could be how *we* want them to be. Would people be upset with us if we could be what they want us to be? So if we can truly learn how to forgive ourselves then we can learn how to forgive others and if we love ourselves and try to love and help others how much suffering would there be in this world?

Sometimes God has to take things out of our lives that aren't good for us. Sometimes we have to go through things that we feel truly hurt by but it is for our own good. It is to help better our lives. It is like a mother who loves their baby. If her baby puts a small toy, or something like that, in their mouth the mother is going to get it out. Usually the mom will grip the baby's cheeks and put her hand in the baby's mouth. This could hurt the baby both physically and emotionally. The baby might start crying because you are taking something they wanted away from them. We do this as adults as well. Something gets removed from our life that wasn't good for us and we cry and complain. But these things are removed for our own safety. God knows what these things well lead to in our lives and he knows if we our going to choke on them. So for our own safety he removes them. Chances are that we will be very upset about it but someday we will understand why it had to happen.

The first step to all of this is learning how to love, forgive and just be okay with yourself. Life isn't about being right or wrong, good or bad or any of those things. It's about always trying to move forward. You need to constantly be trying to better your life. When I say that I don't mean change everything over night, take small steps towards bettering your life, your circumstances. If there is something in your life right now that you know shouldn't be there and is in no way helping your life start taking small steps to removing it. The first step should be to pray about it. Ask God to take it from your life. Ask him to help you and to show you how to take the steps you need to take to move forward and better your life. When I say better I truly mean better. We all have things in our lives that are holding us back from being able to really enjoy life. We have things that we tell ourselves make us happy but really are just helping us cover up our true feelings, making us numb. Do those things really make us happy? No they don't. They make us even more miserable and we get stuck in the spiral of fear and start to hate our life. Just focus on life and realize the things that are holding you back, pray about it, take small steps, and start to change, start moving forward and start to love life all over again or maybe for the first time. Feel peace, feel love, feel joy, feel relief and just live.

Honesty Truth and Trust

The liar lies more to himself
Keeps his treasures on a deceit filled shelf

What happens when you're in a time of great pain or desperate need and no one is there? Usually things continue to get worse but you can always turn to God and rely on him. Ask him for help and he will make something happen that will bring change. It might not come how you expect it to but it will help. Very often it seems worse than the situation you were in but you have to go through things to learn things. You can't change on your own. You can try and you might succeed but for how long? How many times have you tried to or wanted to change something about yourself and failed? How many times have you told yourself "I'll only do this one more time and that's it, no more?" How often have you done it many more times?

Do you lie to yourself and to the people around you? Usually we do that because we are ashamed of ourselves. We lie to hide something we've done. If you feel shame about something or have something in your life you know is effecting it in a negative way tell God about it. God already knows everything you are doing he just wants you to tell him about it. Even if it's something you really don't want to give up or change but know it would make your life better, tell God that. Tell him "I really don't want to stop this but I know it would help me." When people say "Confess it" they truly mean tell him. Just talk to God, he is truly your closest friend. He truly wants to hear about everything. We can't remember each and every sin we've committed and we probably don't know every sin we've committed. You don't have to confess each sin just talk to God and be honest with him. Tell him exactly what you've done, whole heartedly. Don't be like a child lying to their mother. If mom asks "Who broke the lamp?" Don't say

"Well I threw the ball but Billy should've caught it." Don't make excuses, be completely honest. Tell God "I'm sorry I threw the ball in the house, I had a bad feeling something might happen but it seemed like fun at the time." That, of course, is just an example but we need to be completely honest with God and with ourselves. We can't realize our wrongs until we stop lying to ourselves and blaming others for our choices.

Remember that God loves you. He doesn't love you because you are the best person in the world and never do anything wrong. He loves you because you are his child. He wants to help you have a better life. He wants a close relationship with you. He wants you to love and trust him. That's it. He just wants to be loved by you. He wants to help you. In any close relationship you have to be open and honest with each other. God wants you to be more open and honest with him than you are with anyone else. All those deep dark secrets you don't want to tell anyone else you can tell him, he already knows them anyway. He just wants you to be completely open and honest with him. God wants us to be honest with him so that we feel trust in him and can be completely truthful with him. Honesty, truth and trust are very important things to have with God. Just talk to him, open up to him. We don't need to pray in a certain way; we just need to talk to God like we talk to a friend. He should be viewed as the closest friend we have. Not as the parent we are going to upset when we get in trouble. God is our father and everything he does is out of love. God is our friend, our parent, our guide, our everything.

He created this whole universe and what he truly wants is for you to love him.

Remember God created everything. He created us and that includes all of our wants, desires, emotions, needs, fears etc. Satan puts thoughts in our heads that change these things and we start to use them in ways that God didn't intend them for. Now we need God to fix these things. We can't change our own wants and desires but he can. Just as a mechanic can make a car more efficient. He can make it faster, louder, quieter, more fuel efficient or whatever. God can do the same with us. We need to ask him first. A mechanic can't fix your car if you don't take it to the garage. We need to be honest with God. First we need to be honest with ourselves. We need to stop lying to ourselves about who we truly are. Stop trying to be the person we think we should be and just be who God created us to be. Admit to ourselves all those deep dark urges and desires. We can't ask God to fix something if we don't admit that it's broken. Ask God to show you who you really are. We have to get to know us and to do that we need to be in a strong relationship with Christ. He can help us as we discover that we might not be who we thought we were. It can be a very trying and tough time but ask for help and comfort. You can get through it all with Christ's guiding hand. That's when he starts to show his true power. He sets you completely free. No longer worry about trying to be a good person. Just be you. The person God created you to be. God made you and now he is fixing you. He usually does this in steps as we learn new things. Sometimes it's fast but quit often it's a slow process.

In Genesis 3:9 God asked the man "Where are you"? Do you think God doesn't already know where the man is? Of course he does. The man says "I hid myself because I was naked." This is each and everyone single one of us. We are all afraid and naked. Adam didn't say "I ate the fruit you told me not to eat." No, he said "I hid because I was naked." In other words, I was ashamed. The Lord calls to each one of us, though he knows where we are, he just wants us to answer because it's our choice to answer him. Some people who answer his call do what Adam did. Adam hid physically but most of us hide emotionally. We are ashamed of what we've done in this life so we try to hide it from God. We know we did something wrong so we hide it deep in our conscience. Whether we realize it or not it hurts us. It affects us in many different ways. How do we undo this? We have to confess it to God and repent of it, ask for forgiveness. Then he gives us peace and empties our conscience. We still know what we've done. We have to remember our deeds to learn and grow. But that feeling of shame is gone and a feeling of peace is there instead. We can't hide from God. We can only try to hide these things from ourselves. But as long as this stuff remains hidden you can't truly become you. Ask God to forgive you and show you how to become the person he created you to be. Ask him to heal you and then begin that wonderful journey that walk with Christ and be filled with the Holy Spirit. Strap yourself in and go along for the ride.

Most of us are afraid we can't achieve God's expectations. None of us can achieve God's true expectations. We are all sinners but he isn't asking us to achieve those things. He is asking us to come out of hiding. He just wants us to be honest, have trust and feel truth. He wants you to tell him what you've done is this life. Though he already knows, he wants you to be open to him. There are basically 2 ways we can live. One way is to hide from God and lie to ourselves. We can try to hide our sins, our shame, our guilt and our regrets. Or we can be honest with God and ourselves. You can't truly heal until you truly know yourself. The only way to know yourself is to be honest with God and let him reveal who you really are. Sometimes it's a long process. Usually it takes right around a lifetime to learn. But it is an amazing process. It's difficult to bring up your past and all the junk you've done and gone through in this life but it's great to get it taken from you and have that shame and guilt removed.

Think about us as his children. If a parent gets a phone call from their child's school because they got into trouble, most of the time the parent will try to get the child to tell them what happened when the child gets home. They might ask them something like "How was your day today." The child will usually respond with "Okay, same as usual." Then they might make some small talk but eventually the parent will ask something like "Is there anything that happened today that you need to tell me about?" That's when the child realizes that the parent knows something; they realize they're in trouble. They're busted. Usually they still try to pretend like everything is fine. They'll say "Not that I can think of." With a look of innocence that really spells out guilt.

God went through this same type of thing with Adam. Adam told God he was hiding because he was naked, no real reason, there wasn't any major event happening, he was just naked. God says in Genesis 3:11 "Who told you that you were naked?" I'm guessing God paused here, waiting for a response. Just as a parent would look at there child and say "Really, nothing you can think of?" then pause. The child would probably be looking down at this point but not saying a thing. The parent would continue and tell them what they heard had happened at school that day. I'm going to use spray painting the school as an example. The parent would say "I got a call from your school today and I heard you spray painted a wall today." The child's first response would be "But Billy and Johnny were doing it and they said I should to." That's exactly what happens with God and Adam.

Why do parents and our heavenly Father do these things? Why do we all take these steps? I believe most parents want their children to be honest with them. You don't want your child to lie to you. You want an open communication line between you and your children. You want your child to have trust in you. You don't want your child to go through all the same things you went through. You also want them to admit to themselves they did something wrong. If your child is honest with you and tells you what things they are going through or dealing with you can give them advice. When your child trusts you enough to be open with you then you can open up to them and help them get through their troubles. You'll still have to discipline them in some way but try to help them understand why, just as God does with us. When your child is honest with you, you both trust each other a little more and then you can be completely truthful with one another. This is exactly what God wants. He wants us to confess to him what we've done. When we are honest with God we start to trust him a little more, we start to love him a little more. God already loves us and he knows everything we are going through. He is already helping us. He just wants us to open up to him so in return we can become closer to him. Then we can truly start to trust him. And when we are open to him and receive him we also receive his truth. When we begin to be honest with God and trust him we can see the things he is doing in our lives. We can see that he is being truthful to us. The more honest we are with God the more honest we are with ourselves and the more we can receive his healing and feel his strength, truth and power. We ask him for advice and help and he gives it.

Remember we are God's children, which means for us to learn, we do have to be disciplined. If we got everything we wanted in this life, exactly the way we wanted it, most of us would be dead. We wouldn't honestly know how to responsibly handle a few million dollars. Though I'm sure most of us wouldn't mind learning. If we got our wish list answered most of us probably couldn't handle it. I know I'd need to learn a lot before I could. We wouldn't care at all about anyone else or about this world or about children. We would focus on ourselves and that's it, nothing else. But hopefully you've noticed God does supply your needs when you ask, when you pray. So why are we the way we are? Why aren't we content with what we have? Why do we feel jealousy? Why do we want revenge? Why do we do things we know deep down we shouldn't do? The simple answer is because of sin but most of us feel this void in our lives and we will try anything to fill it. This leads us down many different paths in life.

Think about life like that. Think about life as a path or a road. Imagine driving, walking or even riding a bike. When you are doing any of those things you always have to focus on what's happening right in front of you but at the same time you have to prepare for the things that are coming up. When you are driving a car you are watching the car right in front of you but you're also paying attention to what the cars up ahead are doing too. Meanwhile you're looking behind you to see what the cars behind you are doing. If you are driving, walking or whatever you need to know what is happening behind you so you don't get hurt. If you would like to change lanes you need to know where the other cars are. This is life. At all times we have to focus on the things that are happening right now but at the same time we want to prepare for up coming events and remember the things that already happened so we don't wreck. God lets these things happen in our lives to help us prepare for the next step. Don't forget the past but learn from it so you can prepare for the future and then you can take some steps right now to help yourself continue on this journey we call life. Remember the past is paved you can't change it. But the future is a dirt road. Right now we are learning which ingredients we need to put together to make our pavement smoother, nicer, cleaner and clearer. We are learning the things we need to know so that we can have a better future.

In this life there are three paths we can walk on. Each one of us makes the choice of which path we will walk on. You can walk away from God on the non-believers path, you can walk towards God on the believer's path or you can walk with God on God's path. Let's take a look at each one of these separately and figure out which path you are on.

First is the non-believers path. This, obviously, is the path away from God. If you aren't turned toward God you are turned away from him that means you are turned toward sin. If you have no faith in Christ that means you have no faith in God. God is calling to everyone. He wants to help and save each and every one of us. He calls to you and the only thing you need to do is answer. Ask him for help, for change, for forgiveness and these things will be given to you. It probably won't happen the way you think it should but God knows what we need and when we need it. God knows how to help us. Usually it's not easy but it's always worth it. You just have to truly mean it. From the depths of your heart ask God for help. God uses all people to do his will. Remember God created everything and can use what ever he needs to do his will. Jonah is the perfect example of this. God called to Jonah to go into the city of Nineveh and tell those people to repent. Jonah ran from God. He didn't want to do this. But during his time of running away from God he went through trials. The most popular one is him ending up in the belly of a whale. Through those trials he learned how much God loved him. God gave him the courage and the strength to go into Nineveh and help those people. What is it that God is asking of you? What exciting things does he have planned for you?

The second path is the believer's path. This is the path towards God. This is the journey you begin when you become saved. This is the path of sanctification and holiness. You are set free from sin. This is your walk to become more Christ like. We can not be fully Christ like until Christ returns. So your true goal is to be on the path towards becoming Christ like. You want to be continually moving forward to achieve this goal. The disciples are a great example of that. When Christ entered their lives they stopped what they were doing and followed him. They weren't always perfect but they loved Christ and wanted nothing more than to please him. When you feel someone else's love you want to love them back. That's what the disciples did with Christ. Also they knew Christ was God. When you put your faith in Christ and follow him the same happens for you and you become a disciple. And now you can find out who you truly are and what God's true purpose for you is. Now life has meaning. It's no longer about achieving what you think everyone else thinks you should achieve. It's about trusting God, allowing him to love you and realizing his true will for you. When you let God take control you should no longer worry about things. God knows the best things for our lives. What do you think is better for your life trying to do things by yourself or trusting God and allowing him to lead? When God is part of your life you are never alone. He is always right there helping you. Ask him and he will show you the way.

The third path is God's path. God's path is a straight line that never turns or bends. It is like a steel beam. We walk God's path at different points in our lives. Sometimes we are on it for along time and other times only for a split second. To be on God's path we have to be following and listening to the Holy Spirit. When the Holy Spirit is completely leading our lives and we are only following it then we are on God's path. Proverbs 10:9 says "Whoever walks in integrity walks securely." Integrity is confidence, strength, and unwavering in your beliefs that all comes from God. All those who walk with God walk in God's wisdom which gives the ability to walk with confidence and follow God's path. You don't go to the left or to the right but stay on God's path. In Numbers 20:14 Israel wants to pass through the Land of Edom, which is the land of their brother Esau. They were not permitted passage. Even though they promised to stay on one path and not turn to the left or to the right. They had to travel around the Land of Edom-Num 21:4. The people became impatient and spoke out against God. God sent serpents; the people got bit and then healed by a bronze serpent set up on a pole- Num 21:9. This was an example of how Christ was going to heal us all. Because their path was blocked they witnessed a true sign of God's foretelling of Christ. They would have never experienced that if their path would not have been blocked. Remember God has a purpose for all things.

Just as the Israelites were aliens in a foreign land we are all aliens in a foreign land. The Israelites had to ask for permission from the kings of different lands to travel through that land. Sometimes they let them pass through the land sometimes they were rejected. If they were allowed to pass through the land they had to stay on one main highway without turning left or right. We are also traveling through a foreign land and if we could stay straight, on God's path, we would lead a perfect life but the king of this land has his men all around us just off the path. They are trying to sell us everything. Food, drinks, animals, clothes, every need and want we have. Also they talk about beautiful women of this land and their wonderful gods. We try to ignore them but we will turn off the path. Then the king gives us all kinds of things because he wants us to stay in his land. Then God reminds us this is not our true home and if we ask him he will put us back on the path. Then 10 times as many men will come to sell us things because the king of this land is now very angry. When we continue to walk with God we will stay on the path. When we "buy" something or give in to temptation we fall off the path but God will never leave us in this land with Satan as are king as long as we ask him to forgive us and bring us to our true home.

The path toward God does intersect with God's path and at times does follows it but we just can't quite stay on God's path all the time. This is the path God created for you. On this path you are in constant communication with God, just like Christ. When we are walking on the path towards God we are still making our own decisions. The path toward God has many turns and many different roads, lanes, streets avenues and alleyways. There is an uncountable amount. When we are walking towards God we still make many mistakes and take different directions in life. When we follow the path God created for us, God's path, the Holy Spirit is the one leading us and again, we are just following. We know when we our on God's path, you can feel it and life is great. God gives you the things you need to do his work. He provides everything for you. It is wonderful.

Now ask yourself which of theses three paths am I on?

The path away from God, the path towards God or God's path. The path towards God is our goal; God's path is our purpose.

There are also three parts to humans, they are mind, body and soul and when we die the body goes into the earth, the mind and the soul live on. We are conscious after death. We can feel and understand things. Read Luke 16:19-31. If you enter hell you can feel all the pain. You don't have a second chance after you die. You either spend eternity in hell suffering, never ending suffering or you spend eternity in heaven with no pain, no tears, endless joy and bliss forever, never ending bliss. The choice is yours to make. Have a better life here on earth and never ending bliss in heaven or don't. It's up to you.

Always remember one thing GOD LOVES YOU.

Searching for Satisfaction

The eyes are the instruction manual of the mind
What you seek is all you will find

When you are open and honest with God you learn how to be honest with yourself. You learn how to forgive yourself. Don't live in the past with regret and shame. Live in the now and learn from the past. We've all made mistakes. You can't learn things without having experiences. From everything you do in life learn and grow. When you are lying to yourself you are also lying to others. Whatever it is you are lying about will catch up to you. You can't do bad and feel good at the same time. When you try to make yourself feel good you are just searching for things that truly make you feel bad. It comes back to searching for satisfaction. Looking for something that makes you feel good. It could be alcohol, drugs, sex, money or anything. It makes you feel good for a little so you want it again and again and again. The problem is that it doesn't help you. Then you find yourself doing things you never thought you would do to get it again, and for what? It's known as "A cheap thrill." Something that feels good for a little but doesn't last and when it's over you feel worse then you did before you began. What can fill that emptiness that void? One thing and one thing only, God.

All of us are searching for things in this life that satisfy us. We all have this feeling inside of us that makes us feel like we are missing something in our life. There is a void inside of us that needs to be filled. We use many things to try to fill that void. The problem is when we think we find something that does satisfy our cravings that does fill that void; it only satisfies us for a short time. Then we just want that feeling again. Whatever we find that makes us feel good we do over and over and over. It's kind of like putting a band-aid on something that needs stitches.

God isn't telling us we can't do certain things. What he is saying is "Put me first in your life." Not food, not drink, not sex, cars, sports, gardening, your wife, yourself, nothing- put God first. God never said we shouldn't have sex or never drink any alcohol but we need to remember all things are gifts from God and we can't abuse those gifts. Plus, we need to ask ourselves, "Will this, whatever it is, help me improve my life, will this move my life forward?" We always have a choice to make.

Remember that God owns everything and honestly nothing that we have is ours. He gives us gifts. So why do we worry? Look at the things you have and not the things you desire. This world can seem very bleak at times but God has it all under control. We still have to do out part. We need to do what ever it is that God calls us to do. We need to do it by faith. Do all things in faith. We are just the gardeners in his garden. We can do what we want with it but ultimately it is God's and all of it is in his hands. We just need to work the soil. We need to do our job as humans but always rely on God. Always remember that the good things in life are always a gift from God. Think about this if someone bought you a very expensive bottle of your favorite kind of liquor or wine would you chug it down in one day? Or would you honestly enjoy it over a long period of time to respect them for buying that for you? God gave us alcohol as a gift to help us have cheer. He never says don't drink but he does say keep a sober mind. In others words don't get drunk because you do dumb things. Does getting drunk help you improve your life or move your life forward?

Why should we wait to have sex until marriage? That's simple. It hurts all parties involved. In some way sex before marriage does hurt both the man and the women. It might feel good at the time but now you feel a connection with that person. Whether you want to admit it to yourself or not, something is there. Plus, once it's over, you just want it again with whoever is willing to do it. You just try to figure out a way to get it again. Why is that?

Because it only satisfies you for a short time and you want to feel that satisfaction again.

As the Rolling Stones say "Can't get no satisfaction" and it's like that with everything. Take food for another example. Why are the majority of us over weight? We don't eat to be nourished, we eat to be satisfied. We love the taste of food. So after we eat, we search for it again. Just like sex, drugs, alcohol, or even flowers to grow in a garden, baseball card collections, sodas, coffee, shoes, perfumes. Truly we do it with everything. When you like the way a flower looks growing around your house of course 10 more would be even better. I know many women love shoes, just like men love tools. If one set of high heels or wrenches is good, I'm guessing 5 more would be better.

People in general love to point out all the "bad" stuff. I.E. Sex, drugs and rock and roll but it's all the same. Anything we get overly involved in becomes more important than God. That's why the most important thing is loving God more than any material objects, physical needs, and emotional substitutes, more than anything. Love God More than any person, friends, family, enemies, spouses or even yourself. Love God above everything. Anything or anyone that you love more than God becomes your god and then starts to rule your life.

We don't eat to be nourished, we don't have sex to reproduce, we don't get an awesome landscape job done at our house to add to nature, and a woman doesn't put on make-up to look like other women. We want our house to be noticed and look nice, just like we want our face and bodies to be noticed and look nice. Why do we want ourselves and our things to be noticed and look nice?

There are two basic reasons one positive and one negative.

First we'll take a look at the negative. In the back of your brain or deep inside you, you might have some sort of thing saying "Ha ha, I look better than you do" while you point your finger and do a little happy dance. We all want attention and use many different ways to get it. Some of those ways are good some of them hurt others. There is nothing wrong with wanting attention or looking good. Just make sure you aren't putting down other people or having some type of unspoken competition. You will only end up hurting yourself and possibly hurting others as well.

The positive side is that it's nice to add beauty to this not so beautiful world. Don't take me the wrong way God created an amazing world for us to see and live in but our hearts, brains and emotions can cover that up very quickly. It's nice to see a house with some unique landscaping. It's nice to see an attractive women or if you're a women a handsome man. Sadly this is where attraction, love and desire all get mixed up and confused. For example, if you see a burger on TV they make it look the best it's ever possibly going to look. Though you might know that, still quite often, your first thought is "I got to have that." Maybe it's a salad or a sub, whatever, but you crave it. When you do finally have it it's not at all like what you had created in your mind. Usually the same thing happens with relationships. We see a person we our attracted to and the

"Cave man" comes out in us and says, "I've got to have that." If we do get to go on a date with that person after the date we just start thinking about them. We start to make them out to be more than they are. We start to create a fantasy person that the actual person can't live up to. It's amazing what we can create in our minds.

We do all these things for our own satisfaction but it usually only confuses us more. That is why we should put God first. When we put God first in our lives everything else starts to fall into place. Think of taking steps to putting God first in your life as the 4 kings in a deck of playing cards. After God has unhardened your heart ask him to come into it. That's the first king or first step. You move the first king to the top of the deck of cards which is your life. The first king or first step in knowing God moves to the top of your life and everything else gets moved around a little. The more you except God and get closer to him the more he becomes first in your life. The more kings there are on top of the deck of cards the more the rest of the cards will fall into place. The more you mature your walk with God the more he will rule your life and the more things will fall into place. In absolutely no way I'm I saying there are 4 gods. What I'm saying is as you take steps in your life with God he reveals more of himself to you. That moves him to the top of your life and he can put everything else in its proper order.

We will never have complete satisfaction in this world. God has that waiting for us in heaven. We will always be searching for some kind of satisfaction but he is the answer to it. He makes you think twice about your choices and decisions. He helps you look forward and stop looking back. Though we will always make mistakes God will help us through them. Why put God first in your life? To fill that void, to help you get through this life, to show you how to live and make you realize that's the life you wanted all along.

Satan fools us into thinking that we want things that are bad for our lives. I personally was stuck in the trap of alcohol for along time. You feel like that's your only choice. You really think that getting drunk makes you happy but truly it just adds to all your troubles. But that's Satan's game. He wants you to get stuck, to feel trapped and to start hating life. When you get to that point where you feel you've hit rock bottom and feel like the only way out is to end your life, that is Satan. He wants us to give in to him. He wants us to destroy our lives. He keeps telling you how much you need these things in your life that are truly just hurting you. How do you make that stop? How do you start a new life? How do you choose the things that are good for your life? Put it all in God's hands. Look at life in a different way. Remember that the only way to be truly happy is by feeling that peace inside you that only God can provide and when you are truly on the bottom the only way you can look is up. God can and will do it just put your faith in him and trust him and it will all fall into place. He truly will give you what you need.

So what is the purpose of life? In the book of Ecclesiastes Solomon, the preacher, speaks of vanity. What he is saying is that everything equals nothing. Life is nothingness. One of his examples of this is doing work. Like fixing something around your house or helping a friend with something. The award of doing work is mostly feeling good for the work you've done. Think about this, everyone on the planet likes either food, sex, drugs, or possibly all three. But what do we really get out of those things. If they are used for their intended purpose we are nourished, we reproduce and we are cured of an ailment. But then what? Honestly when we have done these things all we are thinking about is how to do it again. And it is like that with everything. Like I had mentioned earlier we are constantly looking for something to satisfy whatever need it is we have. What is the purpose/meaning of life? Let God satisfy your needs and it will last and you will be satisfied. Will you still want things and need things? Of course you will. But you won't feel that emptiness any more.

If life is nothingness why bother trying, why bother caring, why live at all, why not just give up and die?

Always remember this life is nothing because God is everything. God turns your life from nothing into joy. God has a plan and his plan will happen. He will make his plans workout. God has it all figured out and we don't need to worry about anything. The only things we need to do are to keep our faith in him and take the steps he tells us to take. We just need to do his will. Life is never easy in fact it is very difficult. Think of life as our training. God is teaching us and training us how to be his representatives. He wants us to represent him so that we can bring other people to him. None of us deserves the blessings and rewards God is giving to us but it is awesome. So the true question is why go through the turmoil and pain of this life just to end up in a place that is even worse than this life ever could be? Why choose to go to Hell? Why not put your faith into Christ and have a better life now and also get to experience all the wonders and amazing things God has for us in Heaven.

Being Thankful

The one who never thanks just begs
Is the who can't walk though he has legs

We all make mistakes, we're only human, and we learn from our mistakes. We talk to God about the things we've done and he fixes it for us. Why? Because he loves us and God should truly be your everything. Let him know what is wrong and thank him for what is right. Thank him for all the wonderful things that happen in your life. It is very easy to see and feel all the negative things that happen in this life but start to notice all the good things. Pay attention to the good things and thank God every time something good happens in your life and you will start noticing these things more and more. Have constant communication with him.

What does it mean to be truly thankful? In many churches and religious places they can basically give you a list of things to be thankful for. To be thankful for the day, thankful for the food you eat, thankful for the clothes you wear, money you've been given and so on. They tell you to always be joyful, happy, thankful and content in all things. That's wonderful and there's fairies flying around sprinkling pixie dust and we are living happily ever after.

Honestly, this is a dreamland. We aren't happy and content all the time. Yes it does say in the bible be content and thankful in all things. Also it says there will be sorrow and tears. We need to be thankful to God even when we don't agree with what is happening.

Even when we are crying, through tears, try being thankful to him. James 1:2 says

"Count it all as joy when you meet trials of various kinds."

Joy is something that God gives to you and it should never fade. Happiness is a feeling or emotion that comes and goes. Happiness only last for a short time. Joy is always there inside you. Joy is like hope; you can't have one without the other. Joy is something God brings into your life. Remember God has a purpose for all things. Joy is knowing that God will make every situation workout for the better.

Though we can't always see it, God sees the whole entire picture. He knows what we can and cannot handle. Does this mean we should walk around with a fake smile saying "I'm so thankful that life is always so good?" NO, not at all. Just know that what you are going through will change, let God do his work. Remember though things may seem bleak they will always get better with God's help. So basically there are going to be good times and bad times but remember God has it all under control and thank him for that. That is what we should be thankful for, for his help and for his wonderful gifts.

God gives many gifts to us. Some we inherit from him and some we choose to open. You inherit gifts like being an artist, musician, chef, carpenter, things that are natural abilities. God might send you a gift like a spouse but that you have to open. You have to make the choice of going on dates with that person and marrying that person. That is completely your choice. God already knows the choice you're going to make. That probably happened either for your own happiness or to prepare you for something else. It all depends on the choices you make.

Satan sends us bombs. They are all neatly wrapped and look like gifts. We still have the choice of whether we want to open them or not. The difference is that at some point Satan's gift will explode whether we open them or not but thankfully God already has a plan for every gift. Whether it's from him or a bomb from Satan he makes all things work out. This is why we should be thankful. God is always preparing us for whatever might come our way. If we can't deal with it he will. Whatever we are going through God is always there to help, **always**. We just need to let him.

God is there for us because he loves us. Most of us have heard that God loves us unconditionally, like a parent loves their child. We hear that he sent his only begotten Son to suffer, die and be resurrected for us but really think about that and what it means. Have you ever seen those commercials on TV that show the starving children in other countries? It almost makes you cry or maybe it does make you cry. It might make you want to give all the money you have to those children. Whether you do or don't isn't what's important for this example. Maybe you've seen a man sitting against a building, wearing tattered clothing and holding a cup in his hand asking for spare change. These are just two examples but we have all had moments where we have a deep feeling of sorrow for someone we truly don't know. Maybe you see a mother weeping in a hospital because her young child just past away. Either way we know nothing about these people and still we feel deep compassion for them. How does God feel about each and every one of us? He knows each one of us personally. He knows us better than we know ourselves. Do you think he enjoys watching us cry or watching us struggle and go through times of sorrow? Do you enjoy watching your child or any relative go through things of this nature? I hope not. But some things we have to go through to learn, to grow, to mature, not just as people but as children of God. We have to go through things that bring us closer to God and make us mature Christians. You can't become a fully matured adult without becoming a fully matured Christian. Does that mean you become a dull person who does nothing but talk about God and only enjoys life inside a church or other religious houses? NO, not at all. It means to be more like Christ. Was Christ dull and boring? NO. Did Christ confine himself to a temple? No. Did Christ have fun with his friends and just hang-out? Yes.

Should we carry a bible everywhere we go and try to lead every conversation toward God? You can do that, it's your choice. Remember Christ didn't push God at people. He shared God with people. He taught to those who would listen. He didn't run around to people begging them to let him heal them or to let him teach them. When Christ did heal people he told them not to tell anyone else about it. He attracted people through his teachings and people came to him. Where did he usually teach? Somewhere outside, anywhere he could where people were willing to listen. Do we need to be dressed in a suit and tie with a bible in one hand, the other hand behind our back and a smile on our face? Should we try desperately to get people to church? You don't have to. There are many types of people on this earth and to reach certain people takes a certain approach but always remember people don't like being told what to do. Remember religion is man seeking God. Christianity is God seeking man. God wants to save us all but it's still our choice. Try to help people but don't push them to hard. Don't push them away. Don't worry about their past, help them now. Don't judge them, help them. God is willing to forgive us all, can we forgive each other?

Be thankful to God for what you see him doing in your life. There is no right or wrong way to talk to God. Just simply talk to him and thank him for all the wonderful things he has done in your life. Even the things you hated when they were happening but for some reason you realize now they needed to happen. Stop concentrating on what you don't have and be thankful for what you do have. God is there through it all. Ask and he will help. It says in Mark 10:25 "It is easier for a camel to go through the eye of a needle than it is for a rich person to enter the kingdom of God." Love God first, above all things, and always remember everything is from God, don't be proud of yourself. Judas put money above his love for Christ. He was paid to lead the king's men to where Jesus was. The king's men took Jesus and then crucified him. Judas had so much guilt, shame, and felt so bad about what he had done that he hung himself. What is the most important thing in your life? Is it God? Do not be proud about what you've accomplished in this life. But be thankful to God for the things he has given you, the most important being Jesus Christ.

One part of pride is forgetting that God has done everything for you. When you go through hard times and God brings you out of those tough times and things start going better. Maybe you start a new job, start making more money, get a nicer house, get a wife, and have a few kids or whatever might happen. You start becoming happy or like Moses says in Duet. 9:14 "Your heart gets lifted up." Then you tell yourself how good of a job **you** did to get yourself to where you are. Granted you probably did work hard but never forget without God there to help and guide you, you couldn't have done anything and wouldn't have gotten anywhere. Always be thankful and not proud.

Many people say that they believe all things in life happen for a reason. I believe that without a doubt. If you believe that you are saying that there is a God. Otherwise things would just happen for no reason in no particular order. If all things have purpose than something has to be in control. One thing I forget sometimes is God puts people in are lives for a reason and usually it's to help that person get to know Christ. I want everyone to know Christ so I need to, as all believers need to, open up and share the good news with random people. Share it like Christ did, not by shoving it down peoples throat but by letting them know the option is there if they want to know more. Pray before you speak to anyone and, once again, always be thankful for the opportunity to speak about God to someone regardless of how it went. Then let the Holy Spirit take over and pray for that person. They have to make the choice but you can help them along their journey

Expectations

The seeds you plant are the ones that grow
The secrets you hide are the ones that show

*A*t this point, you have sinned, you confessed your sin, you have been forgiven and you ask God to guide you through this life so that you won't do those same stupid things again and again. The problem is that everywhere in life are these little boys named Billy saying "Just throw the ball one more time." There is always that little voice saying "Take on more drink" or "Check her out" or "There's no one watching you can do that." "Just take one little bite of the apple, it'll be okay." This is temptation. Temptation is everywhere and comes in many different forms. Temptation is Satan's game. Satan is constantly trying to lure you away from God and his righteousness. You are not strong enough to win against Satan, at least not on your own. Ask God to help and guide you. Ask him to give you strength. To be righteous is to place your faith in Christ not your own moral uprightness. God wants us to depend on him not on ourselves. What do you think Billy would do if you were just about to throw the ball to him and your dad walked through the front door? He would probably run out the back door. Your father would grab your hand, take the ball and ask you "What were you about to do?" "Nothing" would probably be your response and then it all starts over again. You are punished, you confess, ask for forgiveness, God forgives you and you pray that he will guide you and help you. Of course, you don't change over night. As the bible says, "Put into practice." When you start to think about God and put your thoughts on him, you start to become a new person. You start acting differently and doing things differently but your old self is still there. Now you have a battle between your new self who wants to do God's will and your old self who wants to do what you want to do which is mostly evil. We are creatures of habit and we get stuck in some really bad habits. One habit you might be caught up in is cursing. You get used to the things that surround you and if the people around you say nasty words chances are you will too. It's not the words themselves that are nasty but their function. You don't call someone a bunch of curse words because you're humbled by them or you love them. You do it for one of two reasons. Either to build yourself up, make yourself look masculine, tough and hoping you can intimidate the other person. Or to knock them down and make them feel like they are weaker. However, cursing not only affects the people around you it affects your own heart as well. Cursing makes you feel unclean or dirty. So to cover up that feeling you curse a little more and it just goes on and on like that. The occasional slip when you're upset or just not thinking isn't great but it happens. Don't beat yourself up about it. Pay attention to the things you do as well as the things that surround you. Then you can take those steps to listen to the Holy Spirit and start to change.

I'm sure you've heard people say that as Christians we do not deserve anything God has given us. That is absolutely the truth we deserve nothing. God does not ask us to chase him. He comes to us. He gives us many opportunities to turn to him. We don't have to look for him or hunt him down because he is already there, he loves us all exactly the way we are. He loves us regardless of what we are doing, saying or thinking. He doesn't even ask us to change but shows us how to do it. Think about when you start a new job, go to a new school or when you just meet new people. Not always but usually, we hide things we've done from people. Either for a little while or for the whole time we know them. We are afraid of what they're going to think of us. We are afraid of letting them down and not being good enough. Now imagine you are with a new group of people and you slap them, spit on them and told them to leave and never come back. Then you quickly said "Oh I'm very sorry about that." And they simply forgave you, no hard feelings. God does this for us and much more on a daily basis. As we spit in his face he is teaching us how not to do that. He isn't even asking us to change but just asking us to allow him to change us. We spit in his face and he teaches us how to spit at his feet. Then, eventually, he teaches us to spit at the ground around him, then the opposite direction and finally not at all. In some way, we will disrespect God until Christ returns. We will always be sinners. He says to us give up and I will do it just simply turn to me. Though you have spit in my face, I still love you. He needs to discipline us so that we can learn how to love him and how to be loved.

We are called children of God, sons and daughters of God. We are adopted as sons through Christ. Gal. 4:4-5 says

"We become an heir to God who is the father." We are told to come to God as a child or childlike. We should have the curiosity of a child, to ask many questions and follow the example of our father. So what are God's true expectations of us and why are human expectations so much higher than his are? What are the expectations we have for ourselves?

First, let us look at the word Adult. The definition of adult is grown-up, mature, which we all are. We are grown physically to full maturity and our minds are as developed as they are going to be, whatever level that might be. The word adult and the expectations that go along with that word are much more than most of us can actually live up to. What is an adult by the world's perspective? This is in American terms but everyone in the world wants and expects to achieve the same basic types of things. First, an adult is someone who is completely self-reliant. They are able to take care of themselves and all of their own needs. Most of us, of course, do have the need to have a companion. We want to have someone to share our time with, usually our lives with. This would be a spouse. Once we are self-reliant, we are expected to take care of the needs of others. The steps should be to learn how to live and care for a spouse and the both of you learn how to fully care for a child, though this rarely happens. This is maturing into a full-grown adult, learning new things. For example, we do not know how to love or take care of a child until we have one ourselves. We don't know how to do anything until we do it. It would be great to be able to learn from what other people have gone through but most of the time we have to experience things for ourselves. Maturing truly is just having life experiences and learning from them. That is being an adult but we expect to be able to have a good job, a nice house, a loving spouse, a baby, a dog, two cars, a white picket fence and a nice little nest egg, the whole, so called, American dream. Yet, though we pretend, none of us has the slightest clue what we are doing. Why is that? Why don't we truly understand life?

Let's go back to when we were babies, and don't forget Christ was also a baby. We all were completely reliant on our parents. Then we have life experiences, grow, mature and become more and more self-reliant. As a teenager we feel more self reliant than any other point in our lives. Also, we know more about the world and life than any other point in our lives, at least we think we do and we think we are self-reliant as well. As a teenager, we get our first real glimpse of being self-reliant. Usually we get a job and a car and sometimes our own place to live. Moreover, most of us, regardless of our age, still feel like we are a teenager. We basically feel 17 or 18 the rest of our lives. Of course we have our moments where we realize our age. Maybe because of back pains, maybe our own child's age or because of some circumstance that happens. But as a teenager we get our first real life experiences. That's when we start to learn what life is all about. You no long want your parents help or advice. You want to do it on your own, your own way. At that point the expectations start. What is it that everyone expects of you? That's a question, I believe, we have all had. The problem is that the question actually is what do we **think** other people think we should accomplish. What expectations do you think others have for you? What is it that you think they are thinking? These are questions only you can answer yourself. I believe we all want advice as we grow. But we are so caught up in being ourselves and living our own life that we don't want to ask because we think we should be able to figure it out ourselves. This is trying to live up to man's expectations. We can't achieve these things because we are trying to live up to expectations that we made up ourselves. We are trying to reach expectations that we think other people have. In our blinded eyes, it seems like others are living a great life and "Have it together" but actually, they are as lost as the rest of us. So we never truly grow-up, at least not in the way we describe what an adult honestly is. We are the ones who created the definition of an adult and yet not many of us can reach it. Reaching man's expectations are impossible. We truly are just teenagers pretending to be adults and searching to give answers to our kids so they don't feel the same way we did. We guessed how to get to where we are and now we would like to help are kids or other young people get there a little easier than we did.

The big question is what does God expect? The simple answer is obedience. Personally, I'm not the best at listening to commands or orders so I like to say God expects us to love him. To love him is being obedient. Love him above everyone else and all other things. Once we turn to him and love him he can help and guide us in a way that our earthly parents aren't able to. We can ask for advice from him and he will guide us. He will show us how to live. God never starts to love us, he already does. We have to start to love him. He loves us with all our faults, doubts and negativity. He doesn't ask us to change. He asks us to love him so he can help us change. God wants to help us find us. He wants to help you find the true you. We are all influenced by past troubles, memories, parents, society, the media, teachers, bosses, friends, - the world. God made you to be a certain person for a certain reason. Only through him can you truly find yourself and your purpose. The closer relationship you have with Christ and walk with the Holy Spirit the closer you are with God, the more you live through God the more you become you and the more you enjoy life. That is when you start to change and you see life in a completely new way.

In Romans 12:1 Paul says "Present your bodies as a living sacrifice, holy and acceptable to God." Since Christ was willing to be sacrificed for our sins, we no longer need to sacrifice sheep everyday to cover our sin. But we should be willing to give our lives up to do God's will. We should be willing to forget about our own plans for our lives and be devoted to God always. We can only be a living sacrifice for God if we have no blemishes in his eyes. The only way that is possible for us is by having complete faith in Christ and being born again. To be born of the spirit not just the flesh. Everyday we need to renew our relationship with Christ. We need to worship him by giving thanks, talking to him, singing songs, making writings or by any other ability he has given you. In the city of Jerusalem they had a gate called the sheep gate. This is what they brought the sheep through to be sacrificed. So the question is are you willing each day to walk through the sheep gate? We should all be truly thankful that the Lord is our shepherd and that we are his sheep. If we need to walk through the sheep gate each day to show this and to show our worship of him, so be it. I am thankful that God gave me the Holy Spirit that made me the man, or close to the man, I truly am. God sees me without blemish and I am able to sacrifice myself to him. I am blessed to be his living sacrifice and so are you.

Now, the question is whose expectations do you live under man's or God's? Which would you rather live under? We are the children of God and all we need to do is accept that role, become that child. What is it you want for your own children or the children around you? I would guess happiness, fulfillment and peace. God is our father what do you think he wants to give us? He wants to give us a fulfilled life that is full of happiness, joy and peace. The only way to truly reach any children is by spending quality time with them and teaching them how to live. The only way to be God's true children is by spending quality time with him and letting him teach you how to be you and how to live a life pleasing to God. The closer you become to the person God created you to be, the closer you come to being like Christ. The closer you become to being like Christ, the closer you become to God. The closer you become to God, the more blessed your life will become. The more blessed your life becomes, the better your life and your children's lives and the lives of the people who are around become. When you are a person of God, such as Abraham or Jacob, God will bless you, your offspring and the people closest to you. What more do you want in life? Take a closer look at your life right now and realize all the blessings you have. Realize how wonderful God truly is.

A New View

You can't make honey without first feeding the bee
The man who is blind but thankful is the man that can see

O ur nature as humans is to do mostly evil. The reason we want to do mostly evil is because we have two ways we can live this life. We can have Satan as our master or God as our friend. We choose which to follow. If we don't have a relationship with God then we are following Satan whether we realize it or not. When we do start a relationship with God we see the evil that lives inside of us and we want that to change. We want our new self to truly come out in us. This is our true self, the person that God created us to be.

At this point you start praying to God to help you change your evil ways. I say evil because honestly anything that is part of our lives that we know God doesn't want in our lives is evil. So you pray and ask God for change but your old self is still there constantly trying to pull you in the opposite direction. Plus Satan is there to tempt you around every turn. What can you do? You have to "feed" your new self. The best example of this is planting a garden. You want the good stuff to grow, all your vegetables and flowers. For them to grow well you need to "feed" them good food with soil and nutrients. So for good things to grow you have to feed it other good things but you also have to get rid of the bad things. In your garden you have to pull the weeds so they don't take over. So you feed the good and get rid of the bad. The best way to do this in life is to read God's word. Read the Holy Bible. This is God's word written through man. Every single word in the bible is God's word. God is perfect, he never fails or makes mistakes, which means the bible is perfect and the ultimate truth. Read his word every day and feed the good. Also pull those weeds. Pay attention to the things you see, hear and do. All these things influence you. Whatever is the main influence in your life, whatever your thoughts are on, are the things that will direct your life. For example if your main thoughts of the day are about getting a couple drinks after work that's what is controlling you. I'm not saying alcohol is bad. I'm saying make sure you have control of it and it doesn't have control of you.

Don't feed the old you and your old ways. We all want happiness in this life. When we are doing things we know are wrong it makes us feel bad about ourselves. We start to feel like we are no good. We might have possessions we want but something inside just doesn't feel right. When you're pushing God out of your life you will never be happy. It's impossible to feel happy all the time, but with God in your life you feel good inside, you feel peace and you will have joy. When your new self is doing the things God is leading you to do you feel great. You actually feel new. You feel and experience things you never thought you could. It truly is amazing.

We all need to stop looking at how bad we are and start realizing the changes that are taking place. None of us will ever be perfect and we need to understand that but we have to try to keep moving forward. Not by beating ourselves up but by encouraging ourselves. We no longer can be the person we once where, our old self, but we aren't fully perfect. We are no longer sinners but we still sin. Our actions speak louder than our words. We need to show people how to live for Christ through our actions. We can't tell people one thing while doing another. How do we do that? Live your life between the person you once were and the person God created you to be. Now constantly learn from God and continue to grow. Notice all the small changes that have occurred since you welcomed God into your life. Start setting goals, small goals, for yourself. Remember God changes us. He doesn't do it over night with the snap of a finger, usually it takes some time. Stay in constant communication with him. Pray and read his word, the bible.

Love God, love others, and love yourself. Love God through his love for you. Love others through the forgiveness Christ gave you. Love yourself with the help of the Holy Spirit. Stop hating yourself. You can't love God and others while hating yourself. Which do you think is better? Asking God to forgive you for how bad you are and wishing you could change. Or praying to God for forgiveness and change, and then taking small, tiny, steps to make it happen. God gives you the ability to walk but you have to take the steps. You are no better or worse than anyone else. We are all sinners, and sin is sin. God loves us all, each one of us, equally. So don't worry about what you can't do or what you are doing. Put all of that in God's hands. Focus on what you want to do. Focus on the things you are trying to do.

Why do you want to change? Did you before? You want to change now because the Holy Spirit dwells in you. Now you are fighting between fleshly desire and the will of the Holy Spirit. If the Spirit dwells in you than you are saved, forgiven, born again, you are born of the spirit which means you are going to heaven. You have the spirit of God living inside of you. Remember there are 3 parts to God. God the Father, God the Son and God's Holy Spirit. The Father, the Son and the Holy Spirit these are the 3 parts of God but there is only one God. The best way that I could understand this is by comparing God to water. Think of God as water, Jesus, the Son, as ice and the Holy Spirit as steam. They are all water just three different parts of it. So Jesus truly is 100% God and 100% man. Just like ice is 100% liquid and 100% solid. When water heats up it turns to steam. When God gets excited he releases his Spirit upon us. I don't honestly know if that's a fact but that's how it feels to me. Also remember God made us in his image. We have 3 parts just like God does. We have mind, body and soul or spirit. Our mind is what controls every part of us. Our body does what the mind tells it to because they work together. Our spirit is our 3rd part and very important. What type of spirit you have depends solely on what type of faith you have. Just like God we are 3 parts but only 1 being.

Why do we have such high expectations of ourselves?

The two things God wants us to do are to love him above all things and love others as ourselves. We feel like we are letting God down but all he wants from us is to ask him for help. We can do nothing on our own. If we could do things alone Jesus wouldn't have had to go through all that crucifixion business. All things are done through grace. Ask God to help you even when you don't want to change. For example maybe you enjoy going out and getting drunk. You know you shouldn't but its fun so you don't want to stop. Pray about it and God will show you a new way. Be completely honest with him. Tell him things like "I love sex I don't want to stop but what I'm doing creates an inner struggle, I hate that, HELP ME FATHER PLEASE!!" "I love alcohol what do I do? HELP! I love drugs, cars, food, money, houses, pools, bikinis … etc. HELP ME, FATHER!!!" Whatever it is that you struggle with, from the biggest issues to the smallest, ask and he will help.

You probably won't change in the blink of an eye. I know I struggle everyday with different battles. I feel my inner struggles all the time but God, through the Holy Spirit, will help you. It might hurt. It might not be easy or go the way you want it to; but it will help you. It will open up your eyes to what you really need to be doing in this life. When you begin your walk with Jesus he heals you. Not in a physical way but in a spiritual, mental and emotional way. You feel peace and all that extra baggage you where holding on to he removes from you. Then you can start to see life in a new way. Do you think when Jesus healed a blind man he understood everything he saw right away? Of course not and that is just like our walk with Christ. We slowly start to see and understand new things. Think about a blind man who sees a cloud for the first time. I'm sure that would be very confusing to him. I know exactly what a cloud is because I've seen it my whole life. Anything you experience for the first time can be very confusing and sometimes frightening. That's way God has to teach us to see and understand things in a new way. And always remember God is right there going through it with you.

What do we do? We pray and we ask God for help. Through his word and through life lessons we put these lessons into practice. Learn to crawl before you walk. We give it all to God then take small steps as he gives us the ability to do it. Imagine trying to jump over a huge gap, like from one mountain top to the other. Chances are if you jump you are just going to fall. But if you take God's hand and climb down one side, walk across the bottom and climb up the other side you'll get there. You might slip on your climb, but God is always there to pull you back up.

The bible says many times "Put into practice," not do automatically. That is one of the things this life is about. God is constantly teaching us. He is training us. He is preparing us for other struggles and battles that we will face. God doesn't enjoy watching us go through all of this pain and hardship in life but it's the only way to learn. Don't beat yourself up every time you make a mistake but learn from it. The dumbest thing we do is beat ourselves up for the dumb things we do. Ask yourself why. Why was I in this situation? What could I have done differently? What will I do if this happens again? How can I help someone else that might go through this same thing? There is a purpose and reason for everything that happens.

How different would you view your life if you would remove the words luck and coincidence and instead thought of them as God's purpose and God's guidance. Coincidence can be viewed as God guiding you. Maybe he is showing you that this is where you need to be. This is where he wants you and he is giving you a sign. Were you lucky or did God bless you. When God blesses you it's because you did something he wanted you to do. You did God's will which is your purpose in life. How much would removing these two words affect your spiritual life? You would truly start to notice how God works in your life. God works in our lives everyday but many times we don't notice. We think that's just how things go. We got so lucky that this or that happened and it was so weird how that and that kept happening. We need to truly realize what it is that God does for us and how he works in our lives. Small things can make a big difference. Sometimes God will make big changes in our lives that we notice. But most of the time it's small things that we barely realize. But it usually will start out small and then build into something very big. Like a shack into a mansion. You just need to take a moment and ask God why you are where you are and what he wants you to do. Ask for his guidance and for his help. Ask him for the right words. There is always someone who needs some help and guidance. The best way to help them is to ask God to help you help them and pray for them.

I want to look at heaven in a different way. Heaven, of course, is God's kingdom. In an earthly kingdom the peasants are the people that truly have nothing. For my example peasants are any one who doesn't have faith in Christ. In an earthly kingdom the king and his men walk around and ask the peasants if they will join his kingdom. If they say no nothing really changes. If they say yes the king gives them a farm and the peasants become farmers. The king gives them the farm to show them his love and make his kingdom become bigger. The peasants did nothing to earn the farm. Now they work the farms and try to show each one of the peasants what the king has truly done for them. The only difference between the farmers and the peasants is that the farmers answered the king's call. The farmers try to follow all the laws and rules the king has for his kingdom but just can't do it. But the farmers still love the king because of the love the king showed to them. The farmers want the peasants to see that they are equal, no one better or worse than the other. The only difference is that they said yes to the king. The farmers share their crops with the peasants so that they can taste the seed of the king. The farmer works the soil but the king is the one who plants the seed.

We gain all things through God's grace. The only thing we do to become Christians is love Christ. God gives us everything and we deserve nothing. As Christians we should always be trying to share God's wonderful love with all the people that have not experienced it. Let God plant a seed in their heart and you can just nurture it and help it grow. There are only two types of people in this world, those who have faith in Christ and those who don't. It is that simple. When you pray to God and ask him into your heart he sends the Holy Spirit to come and live in you. When the Holy Spirit is part of you, you start to change. You want better things for your life. Now your body is a temple for God and the things you do reflect him. He, of course, wants you to live a clean life and he will help you achieve that. You will never be perfect but he just wants you to try to keep growing in him. You have to constantly try to move forward in your Christian life or you will fall back to your old ways. That's why going to church, bible studies and meeting with other Christians are important things to do. You need support and advice from other people. If you surround yourself with him your thoughts will be of him. The more your thoughts are of Godly things the better your life will be. When your thoughts are of God and Godly things it changes you and you're out look on life. There are new feelings you have and new things you want to accomplish in life. Some people call these things the "Christian Duty." Christian Duty is a term I can't stand. As Christians we don't have a "Duty" we have a purpose, a reason, we have choices to make. We are asked to be children of God, his chosen people, we are his representatives and we show, through the things we do for others, God's great love. We don't *have to* do these things; we should *want to* do these things.

We, as Christians, are asked to obey God. Which honestly means to love God. We need to build a close relationship with God. That's what true love is. When you love someone, anyone, you want to be close with that person. You want to talk to them, help them and do the things they ask of you. Through loving God we learn how to love ourselves and not be ashamed of ourselves. Through learning how to love ourselves we learn how to love others. When we love others we want to help them because they are in need and we love them. Not because we feel like we have to or that if we help them then God will bless us in return. God knows what's in our hearts. He would rather we hurt inside because we are too busy to help everyone than to do it because we feel like it's our Duty.

Everything in this life is a choice. We choose to love God. The only thing we do not choose is to be loved by God. He already loves all of us. That's why we are here in the first place because he loves us and wanted us to be here for his purpose. When we choose to love him back it leads to wanting to obey him. He then teaches us how to do that. We still have the choice of what we want to do. Do you want to help someone for their own good or for your own good? Do you love God because you feel his love or because that's what you're supposed to do?

If you can't answer this question ask yourself this. Does it seem like you don't have enough spare time to help everyone you wish you could? Do you wish you had more financial support to help those in need? If you argue with yourself chances are you are doing as much as you can and that's great. Unless your argument is something like

"If I give $10 to help this person now that only leaves me with $30 for drinks and fun with my friends later tonight." That's the "Christian duty" talking. Either you love others and yourself or you don't. Helping someone out financially is a hard thing to do. Going out with friends to drink or just grab a bite or whatever seems like fun but what is more important to you. Do you want to have money for things that probably aren't going to truly help you or do you want to help someone who truly needs it? Only you can answer that question. Should you give away every last penny? I honestly can't answer that. Everyone's life and purpose are different. You have to ask God which direction you should go. God will give you what you need for yourself and what you need to help others so don't have anxieties about helping others. Either you can help them or you can't. God will give you things to give to others. Whether that's time, money, food, gifts, words or whatever.

It's never easy watching anyone go through hard times but as humans there is only so much we can do. God can do it all. It comes back to the saying "It's the thought that counts." The more we pray and ask God for help the more he will provide for us. When we need help and pray God might use someone else to help us. If we pray for someone else God might use us to help them. Again we shouldn't feel obligated to help them but honestly want to help them. True Christian love is wanting to help others because we love them. Not wanting to help others because we feel like that's what we're suppose to do.

The two things Christ told us to do are to love God above all things and to love others as you love yourself. First we turn to God and feel his love. When we feel God's love in return we start to love him. He teaches us how to love ourselves. When we love ourselves we learn how to love others that same way. Remember Christ said "Love others as you love yourself." You can't truly love others without first loving yourself. Make that choice. Turn to God, feel his love, learn to love yourself and begin to love others.

Salvation

He blames the past on who he now is
Forgetting the present could easily be his

hy is it that God forgives us?

We all have turned our backs to him. We stuck our noses in the air, turned our backs, spit in his face and marched away. We live our lives in sin. We go against God and everything that is righteous. I'm sure you have seen the verse John 3:16 somewhere maybe a sporting event, a random sign in some audience or just somewhere. You've probably even heard the verse a thousand times. It's like a song you've heard so often you forget how good it really is. Then a couple years go by and you hear it again and you love it all over again. We are going to read and really understand this verse - John 3:16- **"For God so loved the world**- God loves us, all of us, even though we turned our backs to him- **that he gave his only begotten son**- That's Jesus, he gave us Jesus to die on a cross at Calvary- **that whoever believes in him**- the only thing you have to do is have true faith that Jesus is God- **Shall not perish but have everlasting life"** - By having faith in Jesus your sins are forgiven and you will spend eternity in heaven with God. God gave us Jesus so that Jesus would pay the debt for all our sins. Remember Billy? Remember when Billy asked you to throw the ball and your father walked in and caught you both and Billy ran. Imagine your other friend Bobby was there and even though Bobby was just standing there watching you throw the ball he'd take the blame. Even though your father saw the ball in your hand he forgives you because Bobby chose to take your punishment. Then your father tells you "Because Bobby took your punishment I forgive you for throwing the ball and I forgive you for every time you've thrown the ball or will throw the ball, but never forget what Bobby did for you and we can play catch outside so you don't throw the ball and break lamps in here." God forgives you because Jesus made the ultimate sacrifice. He gave his blood, the blood of the lamb, to cover every sin we have committed or will ever commit. All of your sins are covered. You owed God a debt and Jesus paid it in full. And just as the father in my example suggested playing catch outside, God wants to help us change our old ways and start a new life. God will always help us out of our hole, whatever problems they might be. When you ask God into your heart you are saved. What that means is God has saved you from death, from sin, from this world, from yourself, from everything. When you are saved you are guaranteed a place in heaven. When you have truly accepted Christ as your Lord and Savior nothing, I mean nothing, can take that from you. You are going to heaven. You can't get into heaven by being a good person. Isaiah 64:6 says "Our righteous deeds are like a polluted garment." I've also read it as "filthy rags." No one can be good enough on there own to get into heaven. Even our good deeds aren't good enough. Heaven is not for the good, but for the forgiven. We truly are completely lost and disgusting. There is nothing we can do, on our own, to get into heaven. You get into heaven based on your faith in Christ. That is God's plan of salvation. The definition of salvation is the act of saving someone from harm, means of saving somebody or something. The Christian definition is deliverance from sin through Jesus Christ. This is what being "saved" is. Both definitions are basically the same. Salvation is the plan God had for us from the very beginning. God came to help us. I want to use what we were talking about with honesty, truth and trust. We are going to use a child spray painting a wall as the example for the whole plan of salvation.

God told Adam not to eat of the fruit of the tree of knowledge. He told him he could eat of any other tree just not that one. That is were we are going to start. I'm sure your child knows that they aren't supposed to destroy any school property. You might not have ever told them that they shouldn't spray paint a wall at school but they know that isn't okay. If you would get a phone call from the school telling you that your child defaced school property by spray painting some sort of graffiti on a wall, there are two ways you could respond. The first way is to lose control and scream at them as soon as they get home. The second way is to go through the honesty, truth and trust steps. I'm not saying one is better than the other, those are just the choices. With the honesty, truth and trust steps first you would ask your child how their day was. They would respond with "The same as usual." You ask them if there is anything they need to tell you. They realize they are caught but still don't want to admit it. Then you tell them about the phone call you got from the school. They will say something like "Billy and Johnny, my two friends you really like, they were doing it and told me I should to." This is where we try to blame others. We all do this. At this point as a parent you are usually getting pretty frustrated and upset. So you say something like "Ok that's it! No TV, no Facebook, no cell phone and go to your room, NOW!!" Parents usually take away some privileges in the heat of the moment and point their finger at a child who is either red faced and angry, or red faced and crying. Your child might say something smart while they make their way to the bedroom. So the next thing a parent usually says is "Since you're already going to be in your bedroom you might as well clean it up too!!" As the day goes on, usually as a parent you start to feel kind of bad about getting upset. But you don't regret it. Children need to be disciplined. The only thing you truly want is for your child to apologize to you and actually mean it. But there is that feeling of division because you lost your temper and your child won't come give you a hug or whatever. Usually you will go to their room to see how they are doing, and realize they haven't cleaned their room. Maybe they picked up a few things but it was just a half-hearted attempted, and they were probably pouting and complaining the whole entire time. So you either say "I'll help you with this" or "I'll clean your room later don't worry about it." God did exactly these things with all of humanity. God saves us from what we truly deserve, which quite honestly is eternity in hell. The only thing we have to do to be saved is put are faith Jesus. It's a very simple and very exciting step. But don't let me fool you. Once you are saved life is challenging. You need to try to live life in a Godly way. You are now battling yourself, demons you can't see and of course, Satan himself. It's a tough road. But, as I've said, God is always there to help you. It's an amazing feeling to know, no matter what is going on, that everything in life will be okay and it will all work out. That's what God does. He helps you have joy and then he truly helps you through this life.

The plan of salvation starts with Adam, of course. Adam ate the fruit from the tree of knowledge and then he hid from God. Then he told God he was hiding because he was naked not because he disobeyed God. Just like the child with the spray paint. A child doesn't want to tell their parent what they did because they know they will get in trouble, same exact thing with Adam. God says to Adam in Gen. 3:11 "Have you eaten of the tree which I commanded you not to eat." This is basically what a parent would say to there child. They would say something like "The school called and said you spray painted a wall on school property, you know you shouldn't do that." And just like we all try to blame others, whether we are 5 years old or 75 years old, Adam does the same thing. Adam says in Gen. 3:12 "The woman, whom you gave to me, she gave me the fruit of the tree." Adam tries to blame both Eve and God himself for his own mistake. I think this is funny. I can hear myself saying something very close to that. I'm guessing God didn't find it too amusing at that moment but maybe he had a chuckle about it later. Kind of like we do when we retell a story about our kids to are friends or spouse. Truly imagine Adam saying that to God. "The woman, whom you gave me, it's her fault." I think it's funny because I know I've said things exactly like that just with different names.

This is the point where most parents would take away privileges. God did the same thing, of course at that time there was no T.V, Facebook or cell phones so God tells Adam "I was going to provide everything for you but now you have to work the land for food and deal with thorns and thistles. Now go to your room!!" God knew Eve was wrong to. He said to her "Now the man will rule over you and your birth pains will multiple, now go to your room." Just like most parents want their kids to clean their room God wants us to do the same thing. God did this with the Ten Commandments. He showed us what we need to do to clean-up our lives and make ourselves into the people God created us to be.

When you go to a furniture store usually they have pictures of what different rooms could look like. They are nice, clean and comfy. The bedroom suites look amazing in those pictures. If you buy exactly what's in the picture and set it up that way at home it might look like that for about a day or two, for a child I would guess even less than that. God created our "Bedroom," ourselves, to be nice, clean and comfy, to be perfect but obviously it became quite a mess. The Ten Commandments gave us a plan of how to clean it up. Did God expect that we could clean ourselves up? No, not at all, at least not by ourselves. He knew that if we would try at all it would be a half hearted attempt and we would be complaining the whole time. This is exactly what we have done. If we decided to try to live by the Ten Commandments, in a completely self reliant kind of way, we would fail miserably and whine, pout and complain the whole time. Just like we are reliant on our parents to show us how to clean our room, we our also reliant on God to show us how to do it. And just like a parent usually says

"Alright enough I'll just do it and you can help," God did the same thing. God came to us in human form, as Christ, and paid the ultimate price so we don't have to "Clean our rooms." Basically he was saying "I'll clean your room for you and all you have to do is remember I did it and love me for that."

While God's cleaning our room we are standing there shyly feeling like maybe we should help. So with our hands stuffed in our pockets, staring at the floor we lightly kick a ball under the bed and God turns, looks and says "Great job, you're really doing good, the room is starting to look better, wonderful!!" All I would be thinking at this point would be really, I tapped a ball with my foot and it rolled under the bed and you're commending me for that? Mean while God is naming the dust bunnies, putting them in alphabetical order and then sweeping them up and I have a hard time saying "Thanks." I do nothing and you love me. You do everything and I barely give thumbs up.

What I'm saying is all of us are just kids sent to our room. We were all separated from God but through Christ not only were we reconnected with God but now we have the Holy Spirit to help us get through this thing we call life. We are still stuck in our "Bedroom," that is this world and our lives, but God cleaned us up reconnected us with himself and is ready to give us complete bliss. What does he ask from us? Simply to love him, simply answer his call and mean it from your heart and you to will have complete bliss in heaven. You will be saved. Sounds like a good deal to me.

Repentance

A stream is filthy because of what is near
Through filtration it isn't prefect but it's clear

What does it mean to repent? This is a very important question. In the Old testament God tells people many times in many different ways to repent. In the simplest terms to repent means to turn to God and be forgiven. It means to change your mind, to change your ways through God's grace. When you turn towards God you turn away from sin that changes the way you see life. How do you accomplish this? How do you truly turn towards God or repent?

First, we need to talk about what being a sinner truly is. A sinner is someone who is separated from God. We are all born separated from God. What that means is we don't truly know him. He knows and loves us but we don't know him. We are born not knowing anything about God. We are born a sinner. The same as we are born with red hair or blue eyes. And just as we can dye our hair or put in fake contacts, we can try to cover our sin, our separation. We all have that feeling like we are missing something in our lives. We need more in our lives but we do not know what we are looking for. So we try many, many things and we can't find that thing that truly satisfies us. This is when we start to do the action of sinning. We start to put other things before God in our lives and we start hurting other people either physically, mentally or emotionally. We hurt others while we are trying to find what satisfies us. Usually we take these things we have done and push them deep down and try to pretend they didn't happen or we try to do a bunch of good deeds to make up for all the bad deeds but, just like when you dye your hair, your still a sinner beneath all of that. The only thing that truly covers all sin is the blood of Christ. Christ is our reconnection to God.

Usually we turn to God because we do not know what else to do. Something happens in our life that makes us realize we don't really like the things we do and we aren't happy with the person we are. We start to regret the way our life is going. Why do we feel regret? Where does regret come from? We don't regret doing things that helped our lives or someone else's life. You might not be happy about how much time or money you gave to someone but you don't regret it. If you do regret it you did it for the wrong reason or they used it for the wrong purpose. Look at Genesis 6:6. God regretted making man on earth. Usually we regret doing something we know deep down inside we shouldn't have done. Usually we regret sinning. So regret usually comes from sin. But how can regret come from sin if God himself had regret? Regret comes from you making a choice and it not turning out quite the way you thought it would. It wasn't what you expected to have happen. God obviously knew what was going to happen. He did not regret creating man he regretted that he was going to have to destroy what he loved. But he was mainly giving us a great example of what to do when things happen that we regret. Quite simply, fix it. We all make mistakes but its how we deal with those mistakes that make the difference. Things are going to happen in life you don't expect. It could be from something you've done or it might not be. But it comes down to how we react to those life-changing moments. So what is the best thing to do when you regret something or life throws something crazy your way? Confess it to God. Ask Jesus for help and guidance and always keep praying. Be patient, have faith and it will work out.

The first step in reconnecting with God is starting a relationship with Christ, which is turning toward God. What can we do to cover our sin? Put our faith in Christ and trust God. What else do we have to do besides that? Nothing, but when we truly put our faith in Christ we will look at this life and this world in a new way. We will want to do things differently because the Holy Spirit is now living inside us. Remember it isn't about what we are suppose to do but what we want to do now that God has put his spirit inside of us. When you are saved, you are born again and you are now born of the spirit. The Holy Spirit covers your flesh. God has forgiven you for all your sins. Now inside you is the urge to show God to others, to help others. This is the Holy Spirit living inside you. When the Holy Spirit leads life becomes completely different. It becomes a joy. It still has difficulties and pain but with God's help you can handle these things, you can handle anything.

This is part of being born again. When we except Christ as our Lord and Savior we are born again. Obviously, we aren't birthed by our mothers a second time. This is what Jesus talks about with Nicodemus in the third chapter of John. First we have a physical birth then we put our faith in Jesus and we are now born of the spirit. Our old self is dead and our new self has been born. If we go back to the garden example, it is like the end of a season and the beginning of the next. At the end of the season you dig up all your old vegetables and flowers. All the stuff you liked is now dead. Now you have to work the earth, give it nutrients and then plant a new seed so that the good stuff can grow but the bad stuff is still there. Weeds will always grow. Your main focus should be the new seed. The more you focus on it and feed it the more it can and will grow and when the weeds pop-up pull them out. When you are born again God has planted a new seed in you. The life of a Christian is so much like a garden. There is a lot of work to be done to help your seed grow but without God that seed wouldn't even be there, just like us. Without God we don't grow, we do not become mature Christians or even mature adults. And remember this, the best nutrient to put on a field or garden is cow manure. The best way for us as humans to learn things is to go through some tough times. Therefore, the best way for us to grow, just like a seed, is to go through a little manure. It sounds very disgusting but it is true. When you accept Christ as your Savior, and you are born again, you have to continue to nurture your seed. Read God's word, do bible studies and find other Christians to be around. You want your thoughts to stay on Christ. Obviously, you can't think about Christ every second of everyday but the more you think about Christ the less you think about unclean things, the less unclean thoughts you have the less temptation you have. Basically, the more you think about Christ the less you think about Satan. Who do you want in your thoughts?

When you accept Christ into your heart, and you are born again, you are truly just getting started with your new Christian walk. Remember, just because your father, mother, or both were, or are, Christians does not make you one. You personally have to choose to walk with God. The moment you put your faith in Christ you start your walk with God and you are born again. You have had your spiritual birth. You are born again in the Holy Spirit. Now you have Salvation. You are saved by God. Salvation is just another word for being saved. God's salvation cannot be lost. When you honestly ask God to be your Lord and savior you are born again, you are saved and no matter what you do he will not take that back but you have to be in a strong relationship with him. Now you are guaranteed a place in heaven and your name is in the Book of Life. What a wonderful gift. Remember the example I used of the little boy named Bobby who was an example of Christ. Think about this, could you imagine getting in trouble and having one of your friends take the punishment for you. A friend that you turned your back on and you wanted nothing to do with. Imagine you killed someone and faced being executed, actually crucified. Let's pretend we still crucified people. We took spikes and drove them through flesh until they stuck into wood and were deep enough to hold the weight of a person. That is pain. Imagine you faced this and a friend that you had told you wanted nothing to do with ever again shows up and says "I'll take that punishment." This is what Jesus did for us. He took the punishment we deserve for the sins we have committed. He didn't commit any sins. He is God and God is perfect. God loves us so much that even though we turned our backs to him and spit in his face, he became a man and died, and paid for all the wrongs we did against him. He did this so that we could spend eternal bliss with him. God is love. It is our choice to love him. Why wouldn't we love God? Our evil side or old self tells us to rebel against him. That is the true struggle. That is life.

So first we sin, next we realize we sin and want to, or need to, change. Usually, we have to change and God helps us find him. We need to accept God into our hearts. To accept him into our hearts we need to pray. If you want to accept Christ into your heart pray this prayer, just make sure you mean it, do this for yourself and no one else.

- Dear Lord I need you to help me change my life. I know I am a troubled sinner. I need your forgiveness. I believe you died for my sins. Now I invite you to come into my heart and my life. Help me accept your forgiveness and follow you as Lord of my life. Help me give every area of my life to you. In Jesus name I pray, Amen.-

You are now forgiven, paid in full. Go to your bible and read all of Romans but start with chapter 5. In chapter 5 Paul uses the term justified- paid in full. You are now justified, all your sins forgiven, paid, gone. Just as if they were never there.

To sum up repentance it's like this. We are born of our own human flesh into the world that is Satan's domain. We are born sinners because we have Satan as our master, read John 8:44, we are living under his control. Christ defeated Satan and death. When we are born again, we are born of the Holy Spirit in Christ and we become an heir to Christ. Christ is the first, and only, born and receives an inheritance from his father. When we put our faith in Christ, we become part of his family and also receive that inheritance. Through Christ God becomes our true father and has power over all things. No longer can Satan touch us- 1John 3:18. No longer can Satan have power over us and lead us to eternal death. The human spirit or flesh is tempted by Satan but when we our born again the flesh is covered by the Holy Spirit who cannot be tempted.

Inside us the human spirit and Holy Spirit fight one another. We want to do good but have a hard time doing it- Romans 7:19 and 7:25. Thankfully we have a loving God who knows all things and takes care of all things.

The Church

When opportunities are missed a new arises
This is why life is full of surprises

When the church began its whole purpose was to spread the message of Christ. The church was supposed to introduce all people to Christ. The church and its members should help people get through life but not tell them how they have to live. The Pharisees where telling people how they should live during the time of Jesus and the Pharisees had many rules, laws and mainly traditions they made people live by. The church, through Christ, has freedom. People don't want rules and lists of what they can and can't do. If they have these laws and rules they are just going to break them and try to hide the fact that they did it. When you tell someone they can't do something, chances are that's exactly what they will end up doing. People don't want these rules to follow, mostly because they can't follow them. What people want is guidance, help, and they do want love; not dos and don'ts. Basically, people don't want religion. Jesus stopped religion and gave freedom. But now many churches try to combine the freedom Jesus gave us and the dos and don'ts. The church should love everyone. God loves everyone. The church should introduce everyone to Christ and help both believers and non-believers. It doesn't matter what you've done in the past but only what you are doing now. What I mean by that is the past has already happened, that door is closed, now ask God for guidance and rely on him. Let God into your heart and make today a new beginning.

Why were people so attracted to Christ? Why did they flock to him? Because he offered love, he offered a new way to live. He didn't tell people this is how they have to live but offered them a way to figure it out with God's help. He gave me a chance to make the choice. Jesus made it okay for us to mess up, to make mistakes, to be human. But we need to learn from our past so we can grow and live a life pleasing to God. Jesus brought the message of love. Love God above all things, while he loves and guides you, and love your neighbor and treat them as you want to be treated. Everything else Jesus said is guidance for us. The bible is a road map for life. The Pharisees and other men who knew the Old Testament used to say what was right and what was wrong but no one could keep these laws. Jesus said ask God and he will show you the way. What can we do on our own, without Christ? Nothing. What can we do with Christ? Anything. We learn, with Christ's help, how to live this life and love everyone. We truly learn how to live. Not how others think we should live but to live the life God created for us. On this journey of life God will give us what we need to get by. He will give us guidance, help and love. FREEDOM.

Each church has two choices, just like we all do. It can be run by fear or by love. It can tell people what they are doing is wrong and make them leave that church. Or it can introduce people to Christ. When a church judges people and tells them that they have to live a certain way they actually doubt God. God says that through Christ we are all forgiven. No matter what we do on our own we can't ever be good enough but because of God's great love for us through Christ we are seen as perfect. Does that mean we should live life how ever we want to and do whatever we want to do? No, of course not, if you are truly saved God is in your heart and makes you want to do things differently. When you have a true relationship with God you want to do his will and please him. Just like any relationship. When you are in a relationship with a person you want to do things to help them and to make them happy or, in other words, please them. That is all God is asking from us. Plus he gives us, through Christ and the Holy Sprit, all the tools we need to be able to do everything he asks of us. God is asking us to try. He will give us the tools we need to do his will. We need to try to use those tools but he will do the work. God isn't judging you, he is forgiving you and he is there to help you, just ask.

The question is what is God's will for the church? What is God's will for each and every one of us? Jesus says that the most important commandments are to love God above all things and to love your neighbor as yourself. Basically love God above all possessions, friends and family and help others. What is the best way to help someone? Is it better to give someone food or teach them how to plant a garden? Is it always good to help someone? Yes, of course but it is even better to help someone because of the love from Christ that is inside of you. The best way to love someone is to share Christ with them. You can give people advice, you can give them money, you can care about them but if you don't share Christ with them their life will never change. Don't tell them how bad they are; just tell them about what Christ did so that we can enjoy eternal bliss with our heavenly father.

Our purpose in this world is to love God and share that love with everyone else. That is the true purpose of the church. Show people God's true love. Show them what it is like to have peace inside and know that no matter what happens in this life it will all work out for the better. No matter what dumb choices you might make, God can fix it if you let him. Life is choices and all of us are just guessing. We learn from experience. No matter what you have done in this life, God loves you. Turn to him and he will help you, guide you and, most importantly, love you. This is what the church should be doing as well. Loving everyone and helping everyone get to know Christ.

God wants us to represent him. He wants us to bring everyone to Christ. He wants us to be an example for other people. None of us is perfect and none of us ever will be. But we need to show people the love God shows us. We have gone from a sinner who had to change, to a sinner who is forgiven through our acceptance of Christ. If you don't continue to move forward in life as a Christian you fall back. Think of walking up a steep hill. If you stop walking you'll start sliding back down. I strongly suggest reading the New Testament gospels. That is Matthew, Mark, Luke and John. They tell the story of Jesus. They talk about all the things he did while he was here on earth. The things Jesus says are life changing. Make sure that before you start to read anything from the bible always pray. Ask God to help you understand what you are about to read. The more you pray and read the more you will understand. The only thing that matters is God's word. People have said that the bible contradicts itself. That is not only wrong, but impossible. Again, God is perfect therefore his word is perfect. Read Matthew Chapters 5-7. This is the Sermon on the Mount. These are the things Jesus taught. Then read Exodus 20:2-17. This is the law God gave to Moses, the Ten Commandments. People say that these two things contradict each other but they do not. Jesus clarified what was taught in the Ten Commandments. Realize that in the Old Testament God had to teach people how to live. What I mean by that is he had to tell people not to eat raw meat. He had to tell people to make sure food was clean before they ate it. God asked people to sacrifice sheep. This was an example of what Jesus was going to do for us. Sheep were sacrificed when people sinned to cover that sin. Jesus, who was the Lamb of God, was sacrificed and covered all sin so that nothing else would ever have to be sacrificed again.

Prayer and faith are what we as Christians base our lives on. Through faith we believe everything about God is the truth. Though we have many questions we believe because we have faith in Christ. Prayer is how we become closer to God. We ask him for help and give him thanks. For one example read Mark 9:17-25. The man asks Jesus "If you can." That isn't faith. When you pray to God tell him what bothers you and ask him to help you. Don't demand things but ask him. Read Mark 10:49-52. A blind man says "I want to see" and he is healed. He didn't say "Well if you can and you have time for little old me I wouldn't mind if I could see again someday." No! "I want to see." What do you need? Not what do you want, but what do you honestly need. Pray and God will answer your prayer. It probably won't be how you expect it but he will answer your prayer. A few years ago I prayed for change. I didn't like where I was in life and I had no relationship with God. I really didn't know what I needed to do in this life. I got change.

I ended up in prison. That's where God came to me and gave me a new life. He gave me a second chance to start over again. And though it was a very hard road I'm truly thankful I went through it. I needed a wake up call and I got it.

My main point here is that the church should not turn people away, no one! I don't care if you're gay, divorced, drug addict, adulterer or whatever, maybe all of the above. It doesn't matter. The church should be open to all people, regardless of anything. Jesus taught us to love, not judge. We have all sinned and no sin is greater than another. We are all born as sinners and we can't change that. What right do I have to make someone else feel shame or guilt for the way they live? I don't have any right. It's like a pencil accusing a pen of being wrong because it uses ink instead of lead. We all do the same things in life just in different ways. I may have never killed another person physically but I've cut people pretty deep emotionally. Which one hurts worse? I know with some of my own emotional wounds I had wished I was dead. I might not be gay but I've looked at my share of women in an inappropriate way. Society says that looking at women as sex objects is okay but being gay, in most people's eyes, is the worst thing possible because it's just weird. They are the same type of thing. Just remember through Christ we are all forgiven, all of us, if we chose to be. God forgave us why can't we forgive each other? Do we need to let people know when they are sinning? Yes we do. But we shouldn't make them feel shame or guilt. Love the sinner hate the sin. Look down on the sin but not the sinner. In a loving and kind manner let them know what they are doing is sin and that you will help them in any way you can because you love them. This helps us all become closer to God. This is what it says in Matthew

18:15. When you see someone doing anything that is harmful to them or the people around them you have to let them know about it. But be gentle and caring toward them. Think of it like this, when you see someone run a red light you probably aren't thinking about calling the police on them. You just want that person to realize they just ran a red light and never stopped. You want them to know they could have hurt themselves or someone else. That is exactly what you want to do with someone that is sinning. Don't call the whole police force on them and get all legalistic. Just let them know that they may be harming themselves, in some way, and could be harmful to others. And all of us should be able to talk to our fellow brothers and sisters in Christ about anything and feel no shame. We need help from one another, we need advice and guidance. Do not judge but love, forgive and most of all accept people. The more you accept people, just the way they are, the more they will be willing to talk to you and the more you can share Christ with them. You can help them get a closer relationship with God the Father. What is more important than that?

1 John 2:28 says "Abide in him so that when he appears we may have confidence and not shrink from him in shame at his coming." When Christ appears will you want to hide like Adam did in guilt and shame, will you want to run like Jonah in fear, have more love for money than for Christ like Judas did or will you say "Here I am" like Abraham, follow him like the disciples, give into his ways like Paul. Will you be completely overjoyed and ecstatic or filled with dread and loathing? The choice is yours. Will you live in the desires of this world each day and let these doors of anxiety slam you in the face or will you step through the "Sheep gate?" Will you sacrifice yourself to God and live for him each day? Now is the time to choose. Continue on this journey of locked and closed doors or change your course and walk through this unlocked, wide open, welcoming Sheep Gate.

Title Explanation

The title of this book comes from two words in Nehemiah 3:1. It says "They built a sheep gate. They consecrated it and set its doors." In the book of Nehemiah they rebuilt Jerusalem and built a wall around the city. In the wall they built a sheep gate to bring the sheep through to be sacrificed. This is why they had to consecrate it. The priests are the ones who do this. Basically, they bless it, they make it clean. Then as the sheep walk through the gate they are cleansed and able to be sacrificed. Keep in mind that the sheep where sacrificed to cover the sin of the people. You can't use something filthy to make something else clean.

When I read that verse it reminded me of Psalms 23 where David says "The Lord is my Shepherd." If the Lord is our Shepherd than all who believe in him are his sheep. Paul says in Romans 12:1 "Present our bodies as a living sacrifice." So we as sheep who have no blemish because of the blood of Christ should walk through the sheep gate and sacrifice ourselves daily to God. We don't have to be consecrated by priests because Christ made us all clean. His blood covered our filth. What is the sheep gate? Remember Christ is the lamb; we walk into or put our faith in Christ who is our only way into heaven. Christ is our sheep gate; he is our gate to eternal bliss. We give ourselves each day by putting our faith in him and each morning giving our lives to the one true God by making our bodies his, sacrificing our lives for his will. Each morning be filled with the Holy Spirit, pray to God, ask what his will is and for his guidance.

Each morning as you leave your bedroom or walk through some door way, imagine you are walking through the sheep gate. Imagine seeing the blood of Christ laying before you as you give yourself out of love and by God's grace each morning as you take those first steps and enter into his Sheep Gate.

Definitions

Religion- Religion is trying to please God by pleasing man. Instead of turning to God and asking for his help, asking him to show you the way, you rely on man to do it. You have a person tell you what you should and shouldn't do. It's living in fear. Instead of living under God's love you are living by fear of man. You aren't trying to please God you are trying to look good to your fellow church goers or Christian friends or whoever. Yet you have no relationship with Christ. Religion is man trying to get to God. Christianity is God reaching out to man.

Relationship with Christ- To be close to Christ is to trust him and have faith in him. Be completely honest with him and just tell him what you think and feel your weaknesses are. Only he can heal past wounds. Only he can heal period. But you have to be willing to let him heal, willing to turn your life over to him.

Becoming like Christ- To be like Christ is to be perfect. We won't be perfect until Christ returns. Our goal is to be trying to be like Christ. To be like Christ is to have a closer relationship with the Father, God. Christ was our reconnection with God and with the help of the Holy Spirit we continue to get closer to God. The closer we get to God the more we find his will and purpose for us and the more we become our true selves, the person he created us to be.

<u>The True You</u>- We are all influenced by past troubles, memories, parents, society, media, teachers, bosses, friends, the world whatever it might be. God made you to be a certain person for a certain reason and only through him can you truly find yourself and your purpose. The closer relationship you get with Christ and walk with the Holy Spirit the closer you are to God and the more you live through God the more you become you and the more you enjoy life.

<u>To do things through God</u>- To do things through God is to do it above yourself. You can't do anything without God. You can try but it is much better when he does it. That's why life is so hard. When you stop trying and just let God do it life becomes much simpler. Life will always be tough but it's better with God helping you, guiding you and picking you back up.

<u>Freedom</u>- is the ability to make decisions. Freedom is choices. Freedom in Christ is the ability to choose if you want to sin or not.

<u>Slave</u>- Is being told what to do. You still make some choices but mostly someone else makes them for you. When you are a slave to sin you are still making decisions but you are being told by Satan what to do and can feel somewhere inside you what you're doing isn't right but you're stuck and can't change. You are a slave to Satan. You are able to make choices but you are stuck in sin.

Printed in the United States
By Bookmasters